DIMENSIONS OF ENCHANTMENT

By the same author

Parapsychology and the UFO

The Persecution of Mr Tony Elms
(The Bromley Poltergeist)

Manfred Cassirer

DIMENSIONS OF ENCHANTMENT

The Mystery of UFO Abductions,
Close Encounters and Aliens

BREESE
BOOKS
LONDON

First published in Great Britain by
Breese Books Ltd
164 Kensington Park Road, London W11 2ER, England

© Manfred Cassirer, 1994

All rights reserved

First published in 1994

No parts of this publication may be reproduced, stored in retrieval systems or transmitted in any form or by any means, electronic, mechanical, photocopying, recording or otherwise except brief extracts for the purposes of review, without prior permission of the publishers.

Any paperback edition of this book, whether published simultaneously with, or subsequent to the casebound edition, is sold subject to the condition that it shall not by way of trade, be lent, resold, hired out or otherwise disposed of without the publishers' consent, in any form of binding or cover other than that in which it was published.

ISBN: 0 947533 89 3

Typeset in 11/13pt Extended Times and Gatineau by
Ann Buchan (Typesetters), Middlesex
Printed in Great Britain by
Itchen Printers Limited, Southampton

Nadia Mullen (1965-1990)

He broke the Flaming Sword and restored her soul to Paradise. For she, too, had been crucified with Him.

CHAPTER ONE

What would your reaction be if a friend confided in you that he or she had been abducted in a UFO by aliens? Would you advise them to consult a doctor or psychiatrist, or would you refer them to one of the societies that study anomalous phenomena such as the Society for Psychical Research or to BUFORA, the British UFO Research Association?

Medical opinion might be at a loss as to how to deal with so extraordinary a claim so as to return a possibly unjustified negative verdict, casting aspersions on the narrator's sanity, totally unaware of the fact that hundreds of sane and honest people all over the world have reported what most of us would find hard to take seriously.

To start off, a few cases in which I have been personally involved.

The late *Alfred Burtoo* was interviewed at length and passed with flying colours. Then in his late seventies, he lived at Aldershot, where he took a keen interest in the local history and archaeology. Another of his hobbies was angling at night in the sole company of his dog. He was fishing on the canal bank in the early hours of the morning, and fully awake. Suddenly without any warning a bright light appeared and dimmed on the towpath. Two midgets in pale green wearing visors approached. They seem to have been seen by his dog as it started to growl. These figures indicated that he was wanted, and so we find him going up some steps into a craft with a spinning top that strided the path. Once inside, he obediently stood under a yellow light. It was only when they discovered his age (which, presumably, they might have guessed near enough) that he was dismissed as 'too old' and 'too infirm' — they did not say, however, *for what*. On his way back Burtoo noted a glow and a humming noise as of a generator as a preliminary to the UFO'S ascent. He was unperturbed by his adventure and resumed his previous activity, adopting a fatalistic attitude.

Joyce Bowles presents a different profile to the researcher. Sensitively described as a 'powder room attendant', this middle-aged woman's first sighting, in the company of a friend, was of an egg-shaped object which seemed to create some form of electrical interference with the car. An entity in a silver suit, tall, bearded and long-haired, made a short debut. This was in November 1976. They had not to wait long for another similar encounter, when the whole car vibrated to a loud whistling sound. Next they found themselves inside a UFO, though their recollection is not very clear. Joyce was physically affected by this latter encounter which caused a rash on parts of her body. She had to discard her magnetized watch. Her third encounter, when she was on her own, remains a mystery.

Bob Taylor, a foreman forester in Livingston, is the subject of a monograph published by The British Unidentified Flying Objects Research Association. Like Mr Burtoo, he was closely questioned together with others concerned in this interesting case. He came over as a truthful person, and his evidence was supported by external evidence. His employers had great confidence in him. If his tale was way-out, it was no more strange

8

than his investigator's subsequent explanation that he had lost consciousness at the sight of Venus — in the daytime! Taylor was 61 in 1979 and generally respected as a level-headed person not given to hallucinations. At 10.15 am on the 9th of November in a clearing in the forest he observed a dome-shaped object silently hovering above his plantation. The site, which was fenced off immediately afterwards and photographed, is now marked. Two small protrusions like mines, but with spikes, attached themselves to his trousers, tearing them. Police forensic experts were impressed by markings on the ground. Taylor had noted a strong acrid smell before passing out. A man of sober habits, he had no medical history to throw light on the incident. Nor are physical traces confined to this case as we shall show later, making it difficult to explain such events on purely psychological grounds. Not only UFOs, but also their associated effects and proliferations, are a world-wide phenomenon of expanding dimensions. UFOs have been observed on radar. Their most alarming aspects are the ever-increasing reports of abductions. While these are accepted as literally true events across the Atlantic they are, more soberly, regarded as psychogenetic in this country. It would, however, be a mistake to dismiss them simply as products of an over-active imagination.

Great numbers of ordinary folk claim this experience, but its spectral quality sets it apart from the sphere of ordinary everyday perception., There are two main types; 'giants', and small persons or 'dwarves', which sometimes appear simultaneously, but more often as alternatives, but with little or limited agreement if they really come from the same place. Once forced into the flying saucer or its operating theatre, abductees are typically subjected to a medical examination. But this is usually so bungled and absurd as to cast doubt on the expertise of the captors, who have travelled hundreds of light-years for no ascertainable purpose. It is particularly true of the implants that leave scars that would never be tolerated by one of our own 'primitive' surgeons. So also the hypnotic suggestion to make them forget what has happened inside the space-ship is ineffective, since it presents no obstacle to recall.

No one knows what really happens when people are supposedly carried away for the benefit of implausible beings not of this earth. The prelude is often a car-ride along a deserted country road. A frequent mysterious feature is a variety of mechanical malfunctioning, to be discussed later.

Sandra Larson, together with her teenage daughter and a young man, was travelling in North Dakota. At 4 am she heard a thunderous noise and the whole sky was illuminated by glowing orange-coloured objects. Hypnotic regression — the standard procedure in such cases in the USA — revealed that Sandra had been undressed by a mummy-like figure and her stomach x-rayed. She had also been subjected to an operation that had cured her sinus-infection. (This is one of a handful of instances in which actual healing has been associated with encounters.)

A well-known Argentinian artist, *Parravicini*, had been to the theatre in Buenos Aires. He passed by a strange-looking individual and became dizzy and was abducted into a flying machine which he said travelled around the world. This episode had a dream-like flavour. Eventually he returned to the starting-point, and there, still on the ground, was the theatre programme he had dropped. From then on he was in constant contact with the aliens, who assumed the role of Guardians of the Universe.

It may not be irrelevant to remind readers that this happened in the post-second world war period when there was much anxiety about the Atom Bomb which was one of the great preoccupations of that age. To convey an even approximately adequate idea of the multiplicity of the UFO syndrome and its shifting pattern over the years would be a truly gargantuan task. Publications like *Flying Saucer Review* in this country alone have published innumerable tales on good authority. There is the report about a farmer's young son who, on horse-back, was hailed by strangers appearing to be bird-hunters (again in Argentina). They were quite normal in all respects, except that their legs were semi-transparent like the UFO seen by Bob Taylor at Livingston in Scotland. They had those ghost-like elements about them which are far from uncommon with humanoids. They emerged from an elliptical, silvery contraption that stood on three legs, and promised the surprised youngster that he was 'to know the world'. Then they took off at a fantastic speed. A horse and a dog suffered paralysis, while the young farmer was in a trance. If the whole episode was merely imagined by an excitable Latin American, you still have to explain why such reports are world-wide, and why there were three holes in the ground forming a triangle. The Argentinian army, at first inclined to scepticism, had to change its mind by their own sighting of the unexplained celestial object in the same place on that very night.

These encounters are diffused over vast areas without any obvious connection; some people therefore accept them as objectively true and caused by a physical stimulus such as an extra-terrestrial craft steered by the inhabitants of distant worlds.

M. *Masse* owned a lavender field near Valensole in SE France. In the summer of 1965 he was shaken by an eerie experience. It began when he found that some of his precious plants had been stolen. On 1st July Masse started work at an early hour. He was suddenly distracted by a whistling sound similar to the sound of a helicopter. If that was suggested to him, he soon found out that he was wrong, for the thing that had come into view was a machine the size of a car but shaped like a rugger-ball. It stood on six legs with a central pivot. America is fertile ground for abductions. *Three Kentucky women* driving home together shared the unnerving scenario of being faced by an enormous disc-shaped aerial configuration. It unbalanced them enough to prevent sufficient control of the car. They suffered physical effects of various kinds which again is not unusual. There was also a loss of time to be accounted for, another factor frequently associated with such events. Or was it simply a case of mass hysteria brought on by an optical illusion? A leading expert who picked out this case as particularly challenging to the 'All in the Mind' theory, was puzzled and thought fit to warn us against pseudo-explanations that don't stand up to close scrutiny. This is not to deny that the majority of instances are accounted for as subjective and illusive. Even in the minority where illusion can be ruled out, there is no clear, unambiguous proof that anything tangible that could, for instance, be caught on film, is 'out there': the spaceman and his sophisticated flying machine are a con; but who are we being conned by: is it our subconscious mind, or something altogether more sinister? Which brings us to the related subject of witches, elves, and demons.

CHAPTER TWO

A critic of Ufology from America, the late Prof. Donald Menzel of Cambridge, Massachusetts dismissed the whole subject (even before it had become seriously 'contaminated' with aliens and abductions) as a 'Modern Myth'. And so, in a way, it is, to an ever increasing extent. Menzel referred to 'beliefs in demons, evil spirits, the devil incarnate, witches, wizards, ogres, ghouls, harpies, fairies, fire drakes, werewolves, elves, mermaids, leprechauns, minotaurs, centaurs, satyrs, cyclops, unicorns, and chimeras'. Meanwhile the connection with UFOs seems somewhat remote, while his knowledge of witchcraft is rather less impressive, it being simply taken for granted that it is a conglomeration of nonsense. Menzel was a distinguished authority on Astronomy and Astrophysics, but his expertise in unrelated subjects may have been less profound.

Others have since approached the subject from the point of view of psychology, folklore, and psychical research, and made valuable contributions to it. It is a legitimate question to ask whether delusions, illusions, or hallucination can be called in by way of explanation of what may seem to some outrageous claims.

Delusion, according to the Concise Oxford Dictionary, is a process that contains elements of 'imposing or being imposed upon'; a 'false impression' or an 'unfounded opinion'. There is a distinct feeling of malaise about the concept that automatically makes you feel ill at ease. So what about illusions, with which delusion is often confounded? These have an underlying physical stimulus, though the dictionary suggest that here also deception of a kind, if not the very same delusive process, may be at work. At the very least illusions trigger off a false belief regarding the nature of the object or person perceived. The enlightened Renaissance Jesuit von Spee wondered how the poor judge in cases of alleged witchcraft was expected to distinguish between 'the vision and the reality'. At a psychological level, scholars were aware at that time that one could all too easily be tricked by hysterics and mountebanks; in fact, people were then just as paranoid about psychic deception as modern researchers who spend thousands of hours trying to prove ESP and PK.

Mental balance is not negated by the occasional misperception to which we are all prone at times. In extreme cases they may turn out to be as weirdly unrealistic as green angels or cats, and phantasmal sights can be triggered off by obscure processes. These are usually the visionary's 'private property', though some (e.g. the visions of the Virgin at Fatima) are shared by large or smaller numbers. The exclusiveness of UFO abductions is by now familiar ground to be insisted on in these cases.

Few people realize that historically witches of old felt threatened by demonic apparitions to which third parties such as their judges were not sensibly privy. A leading witch-hunter of the time (Rémy) did not consider this fact a good reason for scepticism, since his victims would still complain of demonic attacks when on the point of being consigned to the flames, the Devil by no means looking after his own.

In post-medieval England and America 'spectral evidence' was the lynch-pin in trials for sorcery and compacts with the Evil One. It was two-fold: (1) 'Evidence' that the accused had actually been seen at the gathering called the Witches' Sabbath; (2) 'Proof' of someone having appeared in ghostly form to do harm, usually in the guise of an animal-shaped imp. If in human likeness, it recalls the Phantasms of the Living studied in Victorian times by the SPR, but with the additional element of 'malice aforethought' — a dimension of premeditation rare nowadays in similar accounts. Entranced and possessed, the victim often showed surprising paranormal powers. It is a sad reflection on this dark chapter of judicial incompetence and credulity that uncorroborated accusations, however ostensibly ludicrous, were accepted with a readiness almost beyond belief. Some thoughtful judges were uneasy about contradictory testimony that the supposed culprit had simultaneously been at the 'Sabbath' *and* asleep at home. It was conflicting evidence of this kind that gave rise to misgivings on the part of the judiciary, just as one wonders where the physical body of abductees might be located during their abduction experience — a point on which we have conclusive evidence in at least one case.

To fuel the confusion — it was feared that the untiring agent and cause of all that dismays and misleads honest men and women could by his unlimited cunning fabricate 'sulphurous' impersonations by the temporary creation of a lay-figure defying detection. Even in our own enlightened days there are those who regard UFOs as a diabolic ploy to distract us from the worship of God. Among the religious, Teresa Higginson thought that she was at times impersonated by the Devil himself, or at least by her Guardian Angel. Increase Mather, who was involved in the 17th century witchcraft mania at Salem, Massachusetts, believed that Satan made the witches 'dream strange dreams of themselves and others.' Some luminosities are seen in the bedroom, and suggest the phenomenon known as 'hypnagogic' and 'hypnopompic' vision, when visual impressions are obtained on the point of going to sleep or waking up. More surprisingly, there have been mediums who could externalize more or less solid and life-like figures on a temporary basis.

Some scholars argued that the whole business should be dismissed as a mere delusion and deception, and the good and humane Bishop Hutchinson, who took strong objection to the harassment of poor frail old women as witches, complained of folk being tricked by an 'internal image' devoid of objective reality. At all times, there has been a never-ending quest for the physical component of phantom figures that disconcertingly arise out of nowhere to make their exit in the same mysterious fashion (e.g. by sinking through the ground). If of the spontaneous kind, that simply surprise or terrify, (according to their victims' temperament), they give the impression of being wholly insubstantial; if, however, conjured up by some modern 'Witch of Endor' they may prove indistinguishable from a 'real' person, be tangible, and engage in meaningful conversation. Ufonauts often talk, though some are like rubber to the touch and are notorious for their grotesque features and accoutrement. Going back again to Elizabethan times, a tale told of a supposedly real event illustrates some of the problems encountered at the time.

Since there had been a series of crimes in a certain house that defied explanation, it was decided to keep a night-vigil. The story goes — and you may think that it is pure fiction from beginning to end — that in the early hours of the morning a 'revered matron', the 'most noble lady of the town', was thwarted in the nick of time from murdering a cradled infant. It was no question of mistaken identity. In view of her social status this was 'obviously' a case of impersonation: a diabolic trick to frame an innocent party.

Bishop Hutchinson questioned the legality of evidence given in court which was based on nothing more solid than 'spectral evidence', dismissing it as the 'fantastic notions' and 'sickly visitations' of young 'crackbrained' girls who left the lives of the innocent without any defence. People have seen apparitions throughout recorded history but they are culturally conditioned; in other words, they are differently accounted for at different times and places, particularly in accordance with religious belief. Demonology, which did much to foster credence in terrifying ghosts, declined steadily in the western world in the course of the 18th century with its emphasis on rationalism, at least among the educated classes, who alone had been reached by the enlightenment of the Renaissance which, paradoxically, coincided with the fiercest persecution. Even at that later date there were still old-fashioned scientists like Pontas who 'could not wholly cast aside the authority of the past.'

In as far as hallucinations and delusions were acknowledged, they were considered to be supernaturally induced rather than natural states of temporary psychological aberrations of otherwise well-balanced persons. The Restoration scholar and writer Joseph Glanvill, who so ably investigated a Poltergeist case in Wiltshire (the 'Drummer of Tedworth') still clung to the false choice between ghosts as either the shades of the restless dead or the deceits of 'ludicrous demons', and some of the evidence produced in court (no doubt often in good faith) would raise a wry smile if the implications had not often been so tragic.

One informant saw a lock of wool dimly through a cottage window and identified it as 'white and black imps'; no laughing matter as far as the inhabitant of that dwelling — a poor old crone — was concerned.

Misidentifications — advertising planes as occupied space-craft flying over American towns — are the staple diet of Ufology.

Still, there is always the curious episode relating to that archetypal witch Bridget Bishop, a malicious and terrifying character who practised the Black Arts. One Richard Coman testified that she, together with another, had invaded his bedchamber one night. Coman was in bed with his wife and since a light was still burning, presumably awake. A curious feature of this affair is that these two uninvited and uninviting spectres made themselves available for a repeat performance. One of Richard's relatives joined them to observe at first hand. Not, it is true, without some verbal suggestion the newcomer was strangely affected. The fact that the experience was shared (there was yet another witness) seemed to point to sinister causes. It would nowadays elicit a variety of responses, ranging from curiosity and neutral interest to trepidation and terror. In one exceptional case (to be considered later) the fear inspired in a woman lasted for years; it was a very long time before she could in any way come to terms with it. The phenomenal aspects of the Coman episode are meanwhile worth considering. Except in haunted localities, apparitions are usually seen once only or at rare intervals; to experience the sight of more than one phantom at any time is rare outside UFO-related encounters. A Victorian Census of Hallucinations conducted by the Society of Psychic Research came to the conclusion that where there are several persons present, about one third are likely to share the experience — with the surprising proviso that it is most likely an illusion inspired by a 'real' object. The immediate stimulus may be, it was thought, either mental or verbal suggestion.

In a more recent study at Oxford, apparitions show occasional divergencies to as what is actually seen. This is equally true of the 17th century case reported of Joseph Bailey and his wife, whose psychic adventures contaminated with demonic features are instructive. On their way to Boston, Mass., the couple pass the residence of one John Proctor, then in prison on a charge of witchcraft, when Bailey imagines seeing Proctor looking out of the window, the latter's wife standing in the doorway. This was not a case of *folie à deux* (in which the dominant partner of a couple imposes a perception on the more compliant), since all Mrs. Bailey was aware of was 'a little maid at the door.' Still on their way, Bailey comes across an unidentified female figure, again invisible to his spouse.

Cases of collective percipience of phantoms are not unheard of nowadays. The informant for this tale rightly insists on the quality of the evidence for something possibly paranormal, apparently given in good faith and with due attention to detail; moreover all the more impressive because discrepancies are not glossed over and on the whole rather less sensational and incredible than many well-attested modern accounts of UFO occupants. Were it not for the hallucinated (?) figure of the girl seen by the wife, her husband's adventure into the psychic realm might have been attributed to pathological causes, of which there is some slight indication. On the other hand his failure to see the 'maid' (if physically present at the time) could be diagnosed as an altered perception.

Scholars tended to agree about what causes such false images. Mirandola envisaged 'deceits of the devil' as their origin, where Rémy explicitly denounced hellish 'sensory delusions and glamour', liable to 'disrupt human perception' to the point at which men were sure that they had actually seen and heard what was in actual fact but a figment of their imagination. The authors of the 16th century *Witches' Hammer*, a judges' manual for dealing with suspects, takes the opposing stance that it was heresy to maintain that 'the imagination of some men is so vivid that they actually see figures and appearances which are but the reflection of their thoughts, and then are believed to be apparitions of evil spirits or even spectres of witches.'

But experience shows that visions of this kind are spontaneously generated, and it was realized at an early age that those most eager to see them are least likely to do so — not many of my fellow-ufologists have personally encountered a 'flying saucer', let alone been abducted by alleged extra-terrestrials! In ancient times, similarly, the misguided simpleton who tried to attract Satan's attention was almost bound to waste his time, though the learned Dr Faustus seems to have known what to do. On the other hand, the Foul Fiend and his minions have always had an unpleasant habit of forcing themselves on the good and saintly, inducing horrid shapes and nightmares in their field of vision, and the attacks by incubus and succubus are too common to be ignored in this study, and will be dealt with later.

Squire *Mompesson* of 17th century Wiltshire may suffice as an example of a man of upright character and pluck who became the innocent victim of an exasperatingly disruptive poltergeist who continued to play 'unlucky tricks' on his family. Doors would open of their own accord 'with a noise as if half a dozen had come in and pressed who should come in first, and walk about the house.'

This insubstantial cavalcade, imperceptible to the sight, could all too easily be dismissed as an auditory aberration fostered by the persistent bombardment of the senses by inexplicable happenings, were it not that at another time there was a regular invasion of more solidly perceived phantoms, consisting of 'a great Body with two glaring eyes, which for some time were fixed (upon a servant), and at last disappeared', evidently to everyone's relief.

You may think that this somewhat menacing spectre is not all that different from the more large-scale aliens emerging from their space-craft with dubious intent, and it can hardly be a mere coincidence that Close Encounters are said to be frequently followed by psychic, and poltergeist phenomena, in particular. Mark Moravek in Australia describes several instances, postulating that poltergeists and UFOs may interact in more than one basic way: 'selective poltergeist-like effects' may either happen *during* a UFO experience itself, or else precede or antedate it. Jenny Randle's collection of abduction cases refers frequently to this coincidence with all kinds of paranormal phenomena.

Movarek was thinking of the teleportation of persons — and even of their cars — in certain cases of abductions. It ties up with the alleged aerial activities of the witches.

The archetypal midnight hag (some, however, are depicted in art as attractive girls) on her broomstick has a comic Disney touch about her: a fact which did not always escape earlier students, who were not above lampooning the scenario. But at one time it was a grim reality as far as most people were concerned, even if there was the occasional judge who ruled that there was nothing illegal about flying about at night.

We are considering the supposed phenomenon of transvection, which is closely related to a whole variety of similar subjects (no less controversial) for which there is yet reasonably good evidence. They include traction, levitation, teleportation, bilocation, out-of-the-body experiences (OBEs) and, finally, UFO abductions themselves.

Transvection has a long history in Europe. As early as the 10th century the official policy of the Church was to deplore it as an heretical throwback to heathenism. Mother Church denounced 'wicked women ... who profess that in the dead of night they ride upon certain beasts with the pagan goddess Diana, and fly over vast tracts of country'. In our own secularized age the same object may be achieved in out-of-the-body travel, or by joining the crew of extraterrestrials.

The Church maintained that such things were 'only done in the spirit', and that it was foolish to accept such idle fancies as involving actual bodily activity. However, some seven centuries on Guazzo (in 1626) voiced the opinion, in a rather different climate, that there were occasions when 'witches are really conveyed from one place to another by the Devil, in the bodily likeness of a goat or some other fantastic animal, and are indeed physically present at their nefarious sabbaths.' This was, Guazzo added, moreover a belief 'commonly held by theologians and lawyers among Catholics of Italy, Spain and Germany.' None of these ideas are indigenous to *this* country, though elsewhere (e.g. in 16th century Mexico) magicians were credited with aerial flights. They did not however meet with general approval even in their countries of origin, since it could be argued that they were mere delusions or dreams — culpable nonetheless and, as crimes of intent, deserving of summary punishment, in spite of St. Augustin's disclaimer that he was not responsible for his dreams.

Scepticism on empirical grounds was expressed in the following century by the Italian scholar Tartoretti, who objected that participants in the rites of the sabbath, 'if they feasted at their meetings ... ought to come back surfeited and happy, instead of hungry and tired' and, again, that they should be 'able to escape from prison' with the same ease as they apparently left their bedrooms at night.

Modern critics of abductions have similarly argued

that some of its alleged victims who are reported to have been subjected to rough treatment on board showed no such tokens of abuse on their return, but some late medieval writers enforced the idea that the Adversary could, even in one's waking state, induce vivid hallucinations such as nocturnal flights; as in the bilocation ability claimed of some saints, 'at the precise moment that a man is in one place, nevertheless he is able to appear in spirit in another.' In modern times this is said to occur occasionally with mediums as well as with saintly persons like Padre Pio.

Witches traditionally made their way on broomsticks or some equally improbably implement (cleft stick, distaff or shovel) in a primitive rural culture. More up-market practitioners of the Black Arts travelled on the back of an animal. Basically of course the UFO is a more comfortable and wide-ranging mode of transport, while the sociological context is all too evident. In the early days the application of a flying ointment is frequently mentioned, and it even recurs in modern accounts, though the coincidence may be fortuitous. (Villas Boas had some liquid applied to his bare skin with a sponge — but by that time he was already inside the 'flying saucer'.)

A 15th century prince, as 'illustrious' as anonymous, once persuaded a witch to apply her mysterious salve experimentally, but nothing happened in spite of liberal helpings, although the woman professed great faith in its efficacy. In another case, by contrast, the ointment was allegedly effective. Believers could point to the fact that Jesus had without any physical aid whatsoever been carried to the top of a high mountain; to say nothing of Ezekiel who was conveyed by his hair over a very long distance. (The prophet's extraordinary 'chariot' has often been compared with a UFO.) There was also Habbakkuk. Many divines of eminence — Luther,

Bodin and Melanchton among them — thought that such escapades should not be taken too literally, and that the *spirit* only was conveyed.

In 1560 Giambattista Porta once more demonstrated that the traditional chemical preparations to induce a trance-like state failed to dislodge the actual body of the recumbent subject, but an Italian doctor at least produced the *illusion* of transvection by administering a drug to a control group in a proper scientific spirit. Among those with first-hand experience was the author of the influential *Tract concerning Heretics and Sorcers* of 1536, who had actually handled the ointment.

When it comes to levitation of objects and people, there appears to be good first-hand evidence among much that is legendary, faked and obscure. That 'surprising mystic', Christina of Stommeln, was with difficulty rescued when a cloud suddenly descended upon her and she found herself taken to a different location, the agent in this case having been the Devil rather than the then still unheard of aliens. In 1647 the same agency was supposed to be responsible, suitably disguised as a Master of Arts, for the malicious abduction of a scholar of St. John's at Cambridge. Such abductees always, it seems, eventually return, usually to their point of departure, but the unfortunate young man did not, and only his gown was recovered from the river.

Once again, a man named Harrison mysteriously vanished in 1664. Sadly, three people were hanged for his murder. As it turned out, this was rather premature, since two years later the 'dead' man returned from Turkey, whence he had been spirited away. It was about the same time that a Southwark man could not be apprehended (like Spring Heel Jack later on) since he had the disconcerting habit of just fading away from the midst of his would-be captors. In this he had a very respectable precedent in the prophet Elijah.

Towards the beginning of our own century a young Icelandic medium used to be thrown out of bed, being lifted up and pulled down by an invisible force. He was then forced 'head foremost through the door and along the floor in the outer room'; this in spite of clutching at everything in sight and being firmly secured by his legs by two men. This form of extreme traction was exceptional and of short duration. The dividing line between traction and levitation is a thin one, and in the case under discussion actual levitation is indicated, the boy 'balancing' in the air with his feet towards the window. Of course this is hardly the same thing as being projected into a (hallucinated) space-craft by apparition-like monstrosities for genetic engineering as asserted by American ufologists!

A mistaken belief in levitation was sometimes due to an illusion shared by so disparate a company as saints, witches, and mediums. But the evidence is often quite conclusive. Thus Cotton Mather's patient, Margaret Rule, is said to have been afflicted with veritable bouts of levitation. 'One of her tormentors pulled her up to the ceiling of the chamber and held her there before a very large group of spectators, who found it as much as they could to pull her down again.' This seems therefore to have been a genuine instance of a rare phenomenon for which Mather had gone to the trouble of collecting signed statements. Since no part of her body was in contact with the bedstead, the elevation extending 'a great way towards the top of the room', it is precluded from being diagnosed as the *arc de cercle* of an hysterical fit.

Levitation is also associated with physical mediumship. The evidence in connection with D. D. Home is virtually unassailable.

Among Catholic saints St. Joseph of Copertino is outstanding, the more so as his feats of aerial flight were a source of acute embarrassment to the Church. When it comes to the witches, scholars are wary of giving them credit for anything so improbable and abductees are also unlikely to be believed; or, at least, to have their evidence accepted at face value. Mrs. Hingley complained of being levitated and floating about the house. Mrs. Puddy, in far-away Australia, was actually observed to remain *in* her car during one alleged experience, but perhaps her 'astral' body was bilocated. Incredible? Perhaps; but there is an apparently trustworthy report by a missionary concerning a witchdoctor whose 'spirit' traversed a very considerable distance at night. While his body remained in a cataleptic state, 'something' impinged realistically on the consciousness of a distant native and a pertinent message was conveyed.

It will cause no surprise to learn that such allegations were sometimes dismissed on the grounds that the experient's physical part was observed in a state of deep sleep or trance at the very time of his or her reported adventure in another continuum of time and space. Once more on the border-line of various themes we are discussing, the apparent suspension in space is sometimes due not to the above-mentioned contortion known as *arc de cercle* but to athletic prowess. Still, it is recorded that in cases of 'hysteria-demonopatic' epidemics young girls emulated the agility of squirrels.

Mary Longdon was hexed in the 17th century and was sometimes 'removed out of her bed into another room', or even 'carried to the top of the house' (Glanvill). Typical associated poltergeist phenomena have the imprint of truth; they are often found subsequent to abductions and close encounters.

An official report about a French girl, Francoise Fontain, asserts that she indulged in repeated flights of up to four feet. It required the joint efforts of several men to bring her down. The circumstantial nature of this account inspires confidence. Summing up the evidence, a leading authority on psychic matters (Fodor) says, 'Transportation of human bodies through closed doors and over a distance is a comparatively rare but well authenticated occurrence.' Though few parapsychologists would grant wholehearted approval of such a confidently expressed assessment of the evidence, it is at least pointing the right way in describing teleportation as a 'composite phenomenon between levitation and apport' for both of which there is good evidence.

Sceptics may well doubt whether the Reverend Robert Kirk of Aberfoyle was really carried off by fairies in revenge for revealing their secrets, for in spite of Goethe's evidence, we no longer believe in them. This, however, does not stop us from seeing all kinds of strange and wonderful vehicles. However, there is nothing final about this kind of modern abduction. Nor is it very prolonged; there are no Rip van Winkles in this day and age. According to their persecutors at least, witches could easily overcome physical barriers like walls and doors, and one popular writer, referring to 'the Archives of the Roman Catholic Church', has surmised that 'many accusations of witchcraft stemmed from the belief in strange beings who could fly through the air and approach humans at dusk or at night.' Collective sightings (even in daylight) of weird configurations were neither rare nor necessarily extorted in the torture-chamber. They are not the exclusive property of any one age or culture.

Did not the Prince of Apostles thwart every effort to keep him in prison? We do not hear convincingly of the witches being so lucky, but Victorian mediums seem to have been quite skilled in the art of removing themselves by magic means from one place to another. Thus the Davenport brothers, to quote but a single instance, were 'transported a distance of miles'.

Anthropological data also lends some credence to the seemingly incredible. The above-mentioned African medium successfully contacted by psychic means a native hundreds of miles away and separated from him physically by rough and impassable terrain. De Windt, according to Fodor, knew of a medicine-man who disappeared from his tent while being watched, only to be found unconscious half a mile distant.

Bilocation, once more, must be taken into consideration, in spite of its apparent violation of natural law. It has been defined as 'the simultaneous presence in two different places', with the proviso 'mostly ... in the histories of saints'. Perhaps an updated proviso would say 'mostly in the histories of UFO abductions', but this also is far being an established fact! Abductees are not habitually observed to be physically present in one place (e.g. in their car) while allegedly in another. Under the general heading of religious or mystical bilocation we may also include the adventures of the Venerable Dominica del Paradiso who escaped to a cave where she spent two nights. Her absence failed to attract attention as she was impersonated by an angel: it was therefore not a real case of bilocation after all.

A true example, well attested, are the feats of Sor Maria de Agreda. That lady was seen in two places at the same time no less than 500 times, going as far afield as Mexico where she converted a native tribe. Indications supporting this claim are not mere flights of fantasy.

Then there is the phenomenon of the *doppelgaenger*, familiar to the Ancient Egyptians as the *ka*. This is, once more according to Fodor, the 'etheric counterpart of the physical body which, when out of coincidence, may temporarily move about in space in comparative freedom and appear in various degrees of density to others.' Was this how Alphonse de Liguori in 1774 attended at the death-bed of Clement XIV while being imprisoned in Arezzo? If we could accept Aksakov's tale of the bilocation of a French school-mistress, we would have irrefutable evidence. Closely related to this are OBE experiences which, traditionally at least, involve the concept of the same 'etheric double' or 'astral body', supposedly 'an exact replica' of the physical body but 'composed of finer matter'.

Witches traversing distances by magical means had an alternative mode of achieving this. In the 19th century Col. de Rochas conducted experiments in which a 'plastic' phantom form was created. Induced projection of the 'double' has been reported both in early tests and more recently and the literature on OBEs and NDEs is extensive. The idea was ably championed by a Russian pioneer, Ochorowicz: 'The hypothesis of a "fluid double" (*astral body*) which, under certain conditions, detaches itself from the body . . . appears necessary to explain the greater part of the phenomena.' Henri de Siemiraski, artist and scientist, also stresses the pragmatic necessity arising from his first-hand experience in the seance-room of the 'hypothesis of the duplication of the medium.' (Palladino).

In the case of UFO abductions, the process is invariably *involuntary* and imposed upon by alien intelligences of which one can but be suspicious, both with regard to their identity and their purpose. There are good reasons for regarding them as subjectively inner-created syndromes following a predictably stereotyped pattern, unaccountably anticipated by Science Fiction. The unsuspecting victim is subjected to traumatic experiences under bizarre circumstances involving time-warps and time-losses. All this appears to be triggered off by reputedly geophysical or even quite trivial stimuli. Somewhat untypically, Betty Andreasson encounters non-human beings in a mystical context having been teleported to a strangely symbolic environment.

CHAPTER THREE

With the liberalizing process initiated by President Gorbachev we hear more of events inside Russia. Few people outside that vast country know much about *Voronezh*, a sizable town some 300 miles south of the capital. Suddenly, in October 1989, the Russian news-agency Tass reported the landing of a UFO with three humanoid occupants of bizarre and terrifying aspect. 'Tass', says the 'Daily Mail' laconically, 'is not known for its sense of humour.' Neither, for that matter is 'Die Welt', a leading German newspaper that devoted articles to this sensation in three successive issues, after which it typically lost interest. One of the witnesses interviewed was a school-boy called *Vassja Surin*, whose drawing of the object was shown on 'Vremya', the evening Soviet news-programme on TV. Vassja claims — not indeed an abduction, which seems to be at present unknown in that part of the world — but to have observed the landing of a luminous ball on two legs. He and his pals were petrified as they observed it gliding over a tree. A door opened and something or someone of gigantic dimensions looked out. It was not a pretty sight as the 10 foot creature lacked head and shoulders. Taking its place was a kind of hunchback with three eyes, two fixed on each side and one in the middle. No nose was seen; only a couple of holes. It is all a little difficult to visualize, the more so since the precise details of the sighting are in doubt, the newspaper reports failing to achieve total agreement on all points. Meanwhile the eye-witnesses achieved a general consensus about the height, the presence of three eyes, its silvery shining suit and outsize feet encased in bronze-coloured boots. The 'Mail' mentions a 'giant spacegun' zapping the youngsters who were waiting at a bus-stop. 'One minute he (the creature) was there, the next he had gone.' The original written authority for the incident is 'Sovietskaya Kultura'. Another witness, only a few yards away, became hysterical. The rather distorted humanoid, followed by a robot-like creature, paralysed one boy with his gleaming flexible middle eye while the other fled in terror. After a small interval of time the monster returned to his ship which had been parked on the grass. Both boys recovered as soon as the UFO took its leave.

The local correspondent of the paper was disinclined to dismiss the episode as imaginary, confirming that 'something' had happened. What precisely he could not imagine. Others, like the Yugoslav News Agency Tanjug, were less charitable about this supposed invasion of Soviet territory by denizens from Outer Space — scenarios the Americans and others had learned to live with for many years past.

Unlike ghosts (which they closely resemble) ufonauts do not like to travel except in company. In the West they have been around for a long time and vary a great deal in size and shape. A percipient quoted by the 'Daily Mail' describes the Russian specimens as 9–12 feet tall with 'very small heads', whereas according to another account they were headless. Apparently they went for a walk near their mysterious contraption — their exact number is uncertain — and finally disappeared inside. The surprised and captive audience was 'overwhelmed'

with fear for days. Only one account makes mention of the 'tame robot' that followed on the astronauts' heel, and the 'space gun' is no better attested, though in line with similar tales from other countries.
So can we put it all down to a vivid imagination inspired by too much reading of SF literature? My guess is that there is more to it, and we can meanwhile only look forward to the in-depth investigation on the spot which we have been promised; whether this is going to be in any way conclusive is another matter.
What about the UFO itself? According to 'Sovietskaya Kultura', a red ball 10 cm. in diameter descended from a pink sky in the dark and from a trap-door at the bottom of the machine descended a bevy of humanoid entities. We must make allowance for certain discrepancies as in the number of their entities and their precise description. The Moscow daily 'Selskaya Shisn' speaks of 'red balls' (in the plural) that had made a previous repeated appearance over the city, alleging further that many of the inhabitants of Voronezh saw these, including educated people like an expert in economics, an engineer, and an attorney; probably something (perhaps a natural or man-made phenomenon) was in sight. While the newsagency stuck to its guns, Deputy Editor Igor Jefimov expressed incredulity. But scientists identified the site of the landing and are said to have found 'traces of the aliens'. Genrikh Silanov, head of the Voronezh Geophysical Laboratory, verified the presence of a 30 yard depression with four deep dents in addition to strange pieces of rock. Regarding the latter we are told that provisional analysis failed to identify them and no definite conclusion had as yet been reached. Furthermore, there had been recent sightings of a 'banana-shaped' object. We are looking forward to a Soviet case of abduction, which cannot be far off.
Many aspects of this encounter agree with observa-

tions made in the West, particularly in the USA, and may therefore be regarded as to some extent confirmatory. 'Close Encounters', (a term owed to astronomer and ufology pioneer Professor Alan Hynek of North Western University, USA), are all too familiar to us. As to objects, they are almost invariably described as luminous; often they are so brilliant that they cause conjunctivitis. Some land on four of five pads or legs with clear traces of landing.

The Russian ufonauts are larger than life, but no less convincing than those we are already familiar with, while their reception by the overawed youngsters is what we should expect under the circumstances. Their silver-coloured uniform is almost standard, as is the 'gun' to immobilize the curious. Certain of these monstrosities have previously been suspected of being robots. There is a definite connexion with SF even where (as here) there are no strong grounds for suspicion. Physical traces on the ground are often alleged, but hard to substantiate. (In the Livingstone assault they are well established and photographed.) The unidentified substance of the consistency of rock likewise accords well of what we are told in other instances. John Keel, a leading writer on the subject in America, refers to supposed 'moon rocks' and 'moon dust' that was thought to add weight to the reality of the encounters, but such 'cast iron proof' of superior alien intelligence of advanced technology ('millions of years ahead of us') collapsed when it was found that it was indistinguishable on close analysis from the junk of people's own backyards, and Keel admitted that he 'would hate to go into a law court and prove the reality of ET visitants on the basis of such evidence.'

CHAPTER FOUR

Some have suggested that UFOs have been with us from the beginning, and have written books in which they provide archaeological evidence which is far from unambiguous as far as support of their thesis is concerned. There are many representations of winged and exotically helmeted beings hovering in the sky on ancient Mesopotamian cylinder seals from the fourth millenium BC onwards, but their interpretation is to be sought in the realm of religion and mythology and should not be rationalized into scientific data. The evidence from such early times is just not sufficiently strong to carry conviction.

Ufology as a subject of serious study dates back to 1947 when Arnold saw what came to be known as 'Flying Saucers', a ridiculous name for one of the world's greatest enigmas, perpetuated in that source of much information, 'Flying Saucer Review' (FSR).

Sightings of celestial mysteries predate the middle of our century, and the writings of Charles Forte abound in interesting data of this kind. Entities — nocturnal attacks by them of a sexual nature — and abductions of humans are perennial experiences to which mankind has and always will be subjected, but when ufology became popular in America and elsewhere, these vital aspects proved as great an embarrassment to students as flying friars three hundred years earlier and for a long time they were simply swept under the carpet. 'Little Green Men' are, of course, still a standard joke to the media, as well as a bonus for cartoonists. But the subject often fails to cause amusement, least of all to victims of abduction. Although we are seeking for an answer to this problem, it may lack in reality as all experiences are 'real' in one sense. Hoaxes are comparatively few and far between and it appears as if more people are victims than perpetrators. But hoaxes, you may ask, by whom? A 'Cosmic Hoaxer' like the Hindu monkey-god Hanuman has been suggested.

Attitudes towards the phenomenon have drastically changed over the years and have generally speaking matured into something more sophisticated. We now no longer expect the solution to lie just round the corner. There are some alarming trends which will be dealt with in due course. The 'New Ufology' faces the problems with confidence and diffidence almost at the same time! Strictly speaking, there are no UFOs, but only UFO reports. No one has produced any actual hardware, perhaps this is because there isn't any to produce. It is claimed that crashed UFOs are in the possession of the American Air Force (and have been for some time at Wright Patterson Air Field), including the bodies of their occupants, but this is denied by the authorities. Though this may be a cover-up, it cannot be proved in the absence of concrete evidence. There is good reason for scepticism while the alleged data is as vague and elusive as the spaceships themselves. UFO reports are filtered without exception through the intermediary agency of writers who draw on raw material supplied to them by the experients (i.e. the observers).

It may not always be fully realized that this represents a vital aspect in the study of the subject. Ufology does not simply record: it is a highly emotive and contentious subject whose professors have been known to be swayed by religious beliefs or mere wishful thinking. The concept of Space Brothers of superior morals, technical know-how and intelligence, has a great appeal to the cultist and has even given rise to a new religion. This makes it all the more important to gain information about the investigator as well as about the experient: what is his, or her, psychological background, philosophy of life, and aptitude for impartial research. In short, what are their qualifications and skills? Let it be clearly understood at the start that it is not only the person who originally files the UFO report who must be put under the microscope and be subjected to a process of what Ken Phillips has called anamnesis. Unfortunately such information is not always forthcoming, but a recent American Directory of Ufologists is of some help.

Meanwhile it is possible to distinguish five discrete groups. The main contenders may be classified as follows:

1) 'Nuts & Bolts' buffs, who are more or less persuaded that there are visitors from Outer Space, the so-called Extra-Terrestrials (ETs). In America they are still in the majority.
2) Next in order of popularity are the 'Don't Know's'; the uncommitted who are not at present prepared to put their head on the line and are not sure of the validity of any one theory of the origin of UFOs and their alleged occupants.
3) Proponents of 'natural' psychological explanations.
4) People who espouse a variety of esoteric theories involving concepts like 'other dimensions'.
5) A minority of champions of parapsychological involvement and the evocation of other anomalies.

These groups merit more detailed discussion in the following passages of our study.

The adherents of the Extraterrestrial Hypothesis (ETH) accept it as a rule in a rather unspecified way without caring to pin-point the place of origin of the UFOs. Whereas these used to be located within our own solar system, advances in space exploration have caused them to recede further and further to more remote parts of the universe. ETH is not scientifically established and falls down badly in ignoring the generally agreed finding that it could at best apply to the residual ten percent of genuinely unidentified sightings. While this point cannot be sufficiently insisted on, it does not of course exclude the theoretical possibility that *some* are extraterrestrial. Such a conclusion can be be questioned on other, independent, grounds such as that we are alone in the universe (which we do not know for a fact).

The analysis, based mainly on American sources, shows that a great number of people who have given serious consideration to the problem find the data 'insufficient' to formulate a final opinion, even though the majority of listed ufologists accept the basic reality of the phenomenon, with some veering in the direction of no.1 and no.5, to the tacit exclusion of the single well-established factor that only a relatively minute percentage of reports is significant in as far as it does not simply reflect mistaken identification.

In the study of any supposed anomaly the first step is to rule out 'naturally' explicable causes; that a phenomenon is unexplained is not tantamount to saying that it is inexplicable. In the field of ufology numerous stimuli of apparently insoluble enigmas have been successfully traced. This is also true of the special subject of this study. It remains to elucidate the riddle of the psychological process by which a pedestrian, prosaic stimulus turns into a mind-boggling prodigy, as when a star or plane becomes a manned space-ship with bizarre features. It is an aspect that has not altogether escaped previous attention by students, even if some are satisfied that everything can be adequately accounted for by mundane causes like geophysical factors of obscure origin and nature, at least where simple error is inapplicable as the stimulus.

Psychological parameters predominate and may be considered basic on any reasonable hypothesis, with a substantial subsection devoted to 'psycho-sociological' aspects. Then there are the findings of the behavioural and natural sciences.

Aside from natural phenomena and artifacts (e.g., space-junk), there are the inevitable hoaxes, more particularly the hot air balloons unjustifiably popular with prank-prone teenagers. It is assumed that a 'paraphysical' dimension exists side by side with the straightforward 'physical'. 'Human consciousness' is also sometimes obscurely invoked where the phenomenon is not exposed as simply 'mundane' (e.g. astronomical). And who knows for sure what government and the military are capable of by way of secret research, perhaps including 'anti-gravity' devices.

'Earth-lights' and piezoelectric effects have attracted a lot of attention of late on both sides of the Atlantic. In fact, any combination of possibilities (and impossibilities) finds its adherents and devotees in a field where one is free to look for natural events, psychological quirks, the paranormal, as well as illusions and deliberate mystification and sheer incompetence — all factors to be taken into consideration and likely to create and feed particular types of 'UFO myths'.

It cannot be too strongly stressed that prosaic facts, unusual and little understood by the man in the street, can serve as formative factors. Is there, once more, an invasion of our consciousness by what may turn out to be conjointly 'physical and psychological'?

The whole subject is sometimes dismissed wholesale as a 'new religion', a Cult of Unreason or myth abounding in dangerous delusions and downright 'lies' and deceit; but this is a minority opinion. Meanwhile everyone should be aware of the fact that the majority of sightings reported are misidentifications, though it can be argued that whatever 'imagery' impinges on our perceptual field these arise from an 'objective source'.

Even if we postulate a 'control system' (like Vallee), the prevailing massive sightings of nocturnal lights are suspect as being naturally produced, giving rise to the extension of this insight into their true nature by insisting that all can be explained without recourse to PSI (the anomalous or paranormal), or even by 'cultural' factors. Or one may argue that while one has to concede that one is dealing with 'important phenomena', it is unwise to commit oneself further than that.

Bewilderment arises in the mind of those who embrace *'psychic* intelligence' together with 'exotic *physical* intelligence'. A Jungian approach suggests manifestations from within the realms of the 'collective unconscious'.

The uniquely given evaluation of a 'reality interface' might call for clarification. By contrast, few would find difficulties with a 'multi-causal' supposition — assuming that everything cannot be reduced to mere 'illusion' based on natural phenomena that have created a 'complex myth'.

Additional 'dimensions' are not always easy to conceptualize in the context on account of their inherent vagueness when reduced to catch-phrases with adjectives like 'inter-dimensional' or 'extra-dimensional'.

To explain perceptions as 'psychological' is deemed unexceptional to scientists of all persuasions, but the same cannot be said of attributions to the realm of parapsychology (psychical research). This parameter is most commonly mentioned in passing only, and then often in conjunction with more general aspects, such as 'anomalies'. We come across qualified statements to the effect that 'some' UFOs are 'psychic' while, on the other hand 'anomalous' phenomena are linked with 'mundane', 'natural', and 'secret technology'. Not surprisingly one correspondent to a questionnaire regards them as a 'puzzling anomaly'; another (equally plausibly) as 'anomaly-related mysteries'.

Those who look to the paranormal included exponents of ETH. Exceptionally UFO reports are characterized as resembling 'fairy-stories'. Occasionally there is a marriage of 'psychical and paranormal aspects' in the minds of researchers, but the psychic parameter has not as yet received much attention, presumably because parapsychology lies outside the frame of reference. Conversely, parapsychologists are only marginally involved in the evaluation of our enigma.

One respondent concedes that UFOs are 'important phenomena', while not caring to commit himself further. But what of the 'psychic' intelligences that apparently go hand in hand with the 'physical' ones? It is easier to appreciate that a Jungian approach suggests something from the sphere of the 'collective unconscious'. (It was Jung himself who first became aware of the importance of the subject, which he approached with characteristic empathy.)

Less lucid is a proposed 'reality interface'; while few would quarrel with a 'multicausal' hypothesis — unless, again, all is to be dismissed as an 'illusion', possibly on the basis of natural phenomena resulting in the creation of a 'complex myth'.

Having made a cursory survey of proposed explanations and theoretical considerations, it remains to deal more specifically with some view-points expressed in rather summary fashion, not always aided by obscure terminology.

Even on a superficial reading it will be obvious that there is much overlapping, indicative of the puzzlement inspired by so intractable a subject. And so we find that the protagonists of the (globally) popular ETH may after all *tend* to be rather hesitant champions. Imprecise definition may all too easily result in contamination, while failure to make up one's mind (or stick out one's neck) can be made to look like the much proclaimed virtue of open-mindedness. Some researchers manage to convey an absolute minimum of information and are seemingly hedging their bets; others give away practically nothing.

It is a sad reflection that after more than 30 years of intensive study running into many thousands of pages of print, the data are still considered 'insufficient' to arrive at even a provisional conclusion. Agnostics have even said that we are confronted with 'the unknowable'; a position with which I must admit I have a certain amount of sympathy. There are those who confess to the merest inkling as to the nature of the beast, whether it be 'physical' or 'real', albeit 'indeterminate' or 'psychological'; by all accounts an 'anomaly', or even 'the greatest mystery'. One correspondent specifies an 'aircraft-like' structure (obviously under the influence of ETH speculation), another, in a similar vein, something 'intelligently controlled'. On the other side of the spectrum are the outright sceptics of whom mention has already been made. Not many feature in the American Directory of Ufology, and there are more who admit the importance of the subject *as such*, insisting that it requires 'further study' at the highest level, an alibi for procrastination in forming an opinion eagerly embraced by the wavering uncertain, including the 'sympathetic sceptic' element, and students of what is thought to be 'beyond comprehension' and the minority of the less curious who simply don't care to 'speculate'. Such attitudes do by and large at least represent a welcome shift of attitude from the late Professor Condon's, who condemned further study of the UFO problem as a waste of time unproductive of pay-dirt for the scientific community.

A variety of reasons can thus be given for expressions of non-commitment. Apart from the paucity of hard data and the admittedly indeterminate nature of anomalies, including preeminently the one under discussion, 'many positions' are an option with 'physical' and/or 'psychological' connotations. As to the syndrome as such, however 'real' and 'existing' it may ultimately prove to be, its true nature tends to escape our probing. Again, it is plausible to assume that it may not be one thing and one thing only, but 'multitudinous'. Clearly it has proved 'too complex' to our understanding, embracing as it seems to a wide range and spectrum of obscure 'natural' and other elements. The affinity to other anomalies has often been commented on, including cryptozoology and the 'occult'. It suggest that there hides within its wide range of ramifications an inherent fundamental puzzle deserving, or rather, demanding, the most serious consideration and at the lowest level of assessment 'worth studying'. We must accept the possibility of 'different sources' that make up the syndrome, though the mechanism and the precise nature and function of the stimulus are 'very difficult' to pin down, as there may be 'no simple answer' by only 'many possibilities', so that any one simplistic solution must be ruled out of court. As to the 'don't knows', it is interesting to note that a mere handful only exclude ETH as unsupportable. This is hardly surprising in view of he fact that ufology in its organized form is kept going by belief in ET space-ships. But whereas many proclaim their faith from the rooftops, few indeed profess any inkling of 'whence'. Speculation as to UFO origins range from 'inter-' to 'extra-' dimensional locations to hypothetical 'ultra-terrestrial' realms, belief in 'ancient Astronauts' and ill-defined and ill-conceived attributions to 'alien intervention' from 'out there', One hears of implausible bases on the Moon or Mars, but 'other solar systems' are more plausible and are indeed generally preferred. However that may be — UFOs are considered 'unearthly' and from 'other planets'.

While it is postulated that there is link with 'ancient civilizations' (both real and imaginary!), religion alone has all the answers in its wholesale attribution of the syndrome to 'God's missionaries', not to mention their 'associates'.

The idea that UFOs are from *this* galaxy is really no longer in the running. One thing is certain: ETH will not go away, any more than the syndrome which (it has been said) is going to be with us for ever, although it is fairly outmoded on our side of the Atlantic. It remains in vogue in California and among the backwoodsmen of God's Own Country, with only a single supporter listed as living in the city of New York!

The 'inter-dimensional' hypothesis is not always considered incompatible with ETH. It features as 'extra-dimensional' or 'fourth-dimensional', in addition to 'other space/time dimensions'. 'Parallel space-time' could be an application to ET intelligences inhabiting a 'parallel universe'. Such esoteric realms might escape us by being practically 'unknown', or again they could mystify by their very nature of 'reality interface phenomena.' We could go on indefinitely with much theorizing and confabulation. Is an 'abnormal intelligence' truly at work: a hitherto unthought-of undiscovered 'new dimension'? Has Mother Earth for long been visited by 'time-travellers'? Perhaps we shall never know for certain.

Meanwhile, undaunted by the magnitude of the task in hand, there continue to be those brave souls who are not afraid to speculate on these matters, even if at times with scant regard to the realities or the true state of the art.

CHAPTER FIVE

To return to the case histories. We have held over an account where the percipient is also known to me — and known as an honest witness. In the scorching summer of 1976, a nine-year old school-girl living in a small Welsh village had an amazing experience. On holiday at the time, she decided to go for a bicycle ride in the early afternoon. She was hardly prepared for what she saw on her way. It was a huge silver cigar-shaped object sitting on the ground. Cigar-shaped UFOs used to be seen at one time, but the puzzle is confounded by an artist's impression that shows a *saucer*-shaped configuration. There is a possibility that it changed while observed. The girl's first thought was of nothing out of the world, but rather of a carnival float. But what about the uncannily non-human figure, about 5' 6" high? Here, although she hardly realized it at the time, lies the crux of the whole matter regarding the alleged ufonauts that are supposed to pilot these implausible craft. Although they are in some ways non-human, and sometimes disproportionately large or small and with features more appropriate to children's comics, they are too much *like* us in physique and general appearance to suggest an alien origin; in fact, they recall the 'Little People' or 'Gentry' of Irish folklore. Also, there is the notorious absence of consistency of size and general depiction, as if hordes of ETs are sending us their emissaries, but without any coordination of effort and apparently without any knowledge of each other.

This apparition walked stiffly in apparent imitation of American astronauts on the moon, as if finding it hard to adapt to an unaccustomed environment. We have reason to believe that all this is a sham, as is also the traditional disguise of a silvery suit. Nothing can be taken at face-value. Someone seems to be playing games in pretending to be stranded and taken unawares, when putting on a show for our benefit. The figure had a menacing air about it, but even that was assumed. There again was the usual SF ray-gun. It was aimed at the ground, firing a red ray. The girl was transfixed, but it became clear to her that the ET charade being acted out before her posed no danger, and that no harm was meant. Another phantasmal figure in the tentative guise of a female was to round off the display, and she fled the enchanted scene as soon as she was able to move. By now it had dawned upon her that she had become the object of an 'alien contact' with basically friendly beings, a relationship that so far from terminating at this stage triggered off a series of psychic adventures of an unusual type. However, abduction was not one of them.

We now come to the American classic encounter case involving the Law. It differs in that, as at Livingstone, there are traces on the ground attributed to the legs of the 'machine' and even metallic particles said to have been overlooked by an earlier investigator. The object seen by Police Officer *Zamora* as the primary witness was egg-shaped, and its 'pilots' were at first mistaken for kids working on an overturned car. This shows the typical 'escalation of hypothesis' by which the UFO is at first taken for something familiar, but the identification proves premature and unacceptable in the light of further observation.

Socorro is in New Mexico not far from the White Sands Proving Ground where, after the War, German rockets of the V2 type were tested. The sighting, in 1964, was meticulously investigated because of its special interest and there can be little doubt that something extraordinary took place. Two small humanoids entered the craft while a perplexed Zamora was watching. It took off with an almighty roar, flames scorching the leaves of a tree. An aura of secrecy and mystery was cast over this strange business by the American Air Force, which officially labelled it as 'unexplained'.

Did a space-ship successfully terminate its travel for light-years only to need temporary repair in New Mexico? And why was the supposed emergency successfully concluded at the very moment a police-car happened to turn up at the precise spot? Or was it a military experiment that had gone wrong? Have we been fooled once more by a deceptive display combining superhuman technology with incompetence? Neither theory makes much sense.

America is a great country and its greatness extends to UFOs. Here is a very strange case from Kentucky for which no 'normal' explanation can be suggested if we are to believe the evidence. It must be admitted that it was meticulously investigated. In fact, it had been called 'one of the best-known and best-documented CLOSE ENCOUNTERS'. The location is a small farm near Kelly. There are several witnesses consisting of members of the *Sutton* family to whom a friend reported a UFO. At about 7pm in August 1955 the Suttons' dog started to bark and showed signs of absolute terror. (It is a fact that animals are sensitive to anomalies.) The family of eight can, however, hardly have had an inkling of the sequel, having rather rejected the alleged sighting. Soon the farmhouse was besieged by small, glowing creatures with large round heads whose big eyes shone with a yellow sheen. They looked silvery, and had outsize arms with large taloned hands. As full-blooded Americans the men could not resist taking potshots at these harmless apparitions, but hit by a bullet they floated to the ground and ran away. There was also something very strange and unorthodox about their movements. Their limbs were inflexible and as they fled their arms almost touched the ground. It is not certain how many of these monkey-like beasts were seen at any one time. They moved with extreme rapidity, so that their exact number could not be determined; they may not have exceeded two. What made the whole business so extraordinary and excluded the idea of simians was the undoubted fact that though they were fired on at close range the bullets made no impact on them and it was eventually decided to leave well alone. They were shy of light and always approached from the dark side of the house.

One of the earliest accounts of an alleged abduction in England was at Aveley in Essex. It was originally reported in the *Flying Saucer Review*. When I interviewed Mr *John Day*, in 1988, he complained of having been misrepresented. This case set a trend in being probed under hypnosis, the first of its kind in this country. It has since been established that hypnotic regression is a two-edged sword. John and his wife Sue were returning to their Essex village from a visit to relatives towards the end of October 1947. It all started off at 10.20 pm characteristically with a blue light in the sky. Whatever it may have been (and no stimulus is too trivial or commonplace to trigger off profound and deep evocation in the mind), was dismissed by the family until they drove into a patch of green mist that made their radio spark. When they finally got home they thought that they had lost two and a half hours on their journey; again typical of Close Encounters. The experience caused a complete change of life-style, and among other things the Days became vegetarians. He used to have several people working for him prior to 1947, which implies a certain measure of success and prosperity rather than the more reduced circumstances that had been attributed to him. There was, however, nothing traumatic about his abduction: on the contrary, it was the most marvellous thing that had ever happened to him, the suggestion being that it had been of the nature of a religious conversion. The beneficial result was that he had stopped chain-smoking and drinking, plus his newly found revulsion to meat. One had the impression that, in common with others one has listened to, he was withholding something too sacred and personal to be revealed to all and sundry, he being slightly vague in his description. He was not a believer in ETH. As to his psychological state, there could have been a trace of paranoia and I was not surprised that he claimed a number of psychical happenings including psychokinetic movements of objects and seeing apparitions.

Notwithstanding Day's general enthusiasm, both he and his wife complained of unpleasant side-effects like nightmares and being haunted by certain repugnant small creatures. These led to hypnotic regression by a London dentist during which it emerged that Sue had floated out of the car into the UFO while at the same time being inside her own vehicle. (This was observed to have happened in the case of Mrs. *Puddy* whose physical body never left the car she was travelling in.) Once in the UFO, husband and wife were subjected to the standard medical examination which features so prominently (not to say monotonously) in subsequent reports. Tall, helmeted aliens in silvery suits posed as doctors and surgeons. They are described as fair-skinned with large almond-shaped eyes. As a timely concession to modern technology the Days were obliged (or privileged) to inspect the engine-room, where they were treated to videos and holograms. The purpose of the medical examination was rather significantly couched in terms of genetic engineering in addition with interference with the memory of the supposed manipulation. Another preoccupation of the period surfaced when John was shown a picture of our planet after its destruction by pollution. The whole weird scenario owed not a little to SF with it transparent element and suggestions of the obsessions prevalent at the time.

A later incident from England that still predates that American debut of the abduction syndrome of 1963 (the *Hill* story) takes us no further afield than Wotton in Surrey. The date is 1954, but it comes to light 30 years later, and then by the merest of chances. There is no explicit connexion with UFOs and, when details were eventually published the investigators wrote it up as retrocognition in line with that famous classic, the Versailles Adventure of Miss Moberly and Miss Jourdan. The Wotton incident would not be unique in relating to a close encounter in which there is no actual mention of the presence of a UFO, while recording the attendance of strange phantasmal entities attributed to extra-terrestrial origin.

One morning in the summer of 1954 Mr and Mrs '*Allan*' decided to take a day off for a relaxing ramble among the Surrey hills, being in a state of exhaustion due to overwork. They also suffered from a sensation of unusual depression. Though quite at home in that neck of the woods they missed the bus-stop to go on to the next, which was Wotton Hatch. Here they were drawn to the local church with its historic tombs and inscriptions. When they finally settled down for a sandwich lunch they noted with surprise that it was already noon, for they had set out early that morning. An aura of unreality pervaded the whole scene. It had a devastating effect on the woman, who shivered and panicked for no obvious reason. Through the back of her head she became aware of the presence of sinister figures in black. Could there have been a connection with the mythical *Men in Black* reported in some contemporary American cases?

However that may be — and at this stage it can only be claimed as a passing thought — Mrs Allan was by that time in the grip of paralysis and feeling intensely cold. Having made their escape from that inhospitable site, the couple fell asleep on the grass.

The memory of their journey home is of the vaguest; Mr. Allan was also affected by this mood of 'fatigue and amnesia', but apparently not to anything like the same degree. When, two years on, Mrs. Allan had at long last overcome her intense feeling of horror, the very landscape as recalled by her had simply disappeared into thin air, together with the wooden seat on which they had taken their picnic. 35 years later no shred of evidence has come to light that there is any tradition of haunting at Wotton.

The case is minutely researched, but the interpretation of the data is less certain. UFO abductions were still a thing of the future. The original investigators were competent, as were those who followed up the case with field investigation on the spot. But they thought in terms of a *straightforward* case of haunting of the retrocognitive type, although many features point in another direction. What first alerted me to the possibility of an alternative view was the implied suggestion of Missing Time, which hardly ever fails to present itself in Ufology. It is slightly odd, to say the least, that the Allans went past their intended goal in familiar terrain, and their subsequent adventures are marked by a degree of non-realism pointing not so much to confabulation as to a shared altered state of mind.

A similar trance-state was apparent in the case of the *two Oxford dons*, whose experiences also did not totally tally. As will be remembered, the two ladies were allegedly transplanted into a time-warp at the Petit Trianon in which their whole perceptions were altered. It is therefore not surprising that a close parallel with Versailles should have suggested itself. But although there are several points of contact between the two cases, the differences are no less notable. A number of these spring to mind: Apparitions *usually* occur near one's home or inside it. Drowsiness and 'visual disturbances' are typical of UFO cases, though not exclusively so. Paralysis (rare in apparitional cases) is a standard feature in Close Encounters. An 'introductory eerie silence' and the shutting out of natural sounds typically precede encounters with aliens and related experiences. Plurality of entities in a single sighting is indicative of a UFO incident. Missing Time (time-lapses and warps) is the recognized hallmark of the syndrome.

Whatever may be their true nature or significance, abductions tend to include this traumatic element, whereas the occasional glimpse of the psychic dimension as studied in the chronicles of paranormal research are usually easily accommodated by the percipient. Mild interest, or even slight amusement, are frequent reactions to an experience that may even be laughed off as a mere coincidence, trick of the light, or illusion. Not so in the case under discussion. Mrs. Allan, who escaped the additional complications resulting from hypnotic regression (not in vogue at that time), suffered long and in silence, and even leading experts in the field caused disappointment for reasons beyond their control. Like many others before and after her, she may have feared scepticism, if not outright ridicule, and so chose to hide behind a pseudonym. Like Dante, she had suffered something seemingly beyond comprehension, a trauma 'which even in recall' renewed her fear, 'so bitter — death is hardly more severe!'

The idea of a UFO experience without an actual sighting may seem a contradiction in itself, but it is really all a question of definition and conception of the phenomenon as such. A dogmatic but unsoundly founded faith in UFOs as expressing superior alien technology may dismiss the very idea as absurd, but to those aware of other aspects of the enigma (e.g. its parapsychological one) it is certainly worth considering.

An example of an unquestioned Close Encounter from America where no structured object is described and where no aliens or ufonauts figure may be summarized as follows.

A *middle-aged couple* were going by car in California on an hour's journey over familiar ground. It is another of those cases where what Prof. Hynek has termed 'escalation of hypothesis' is much to the fore. The wife saw directly ahead what seemed to be a bright star, but when it 'turned blue' she changed her mind and reconsidered that it was a plane or helicopter. It was now also noticed by her husband, meanwhile changing its colour to pink. At the same time it got larger and, she presumed, closer. In another change of colour (to yellow-white) it 'became huge' and a collision seemed imminent. She was now certain that it was an airliner, but since the light was (typically) 'blinding' she failed to see it distinctly. Whatever it was then changed direction, noiselessly and eventually disappeared. As so often here the road was deserted, though we are not told whether or not it was normally a busy one. By the time they got home two hours had elapsed, and they could not account for the loss of a whole hour. This case thus agrees with the preceding one in that the couple reported no clearly-shaped configuration; but there was this tremendous light. Mrs. Allan, on the other hand, saw human-shaped figures in black, somewhat similar to the mysterious Men In Black (MIBs) of American ufology, which we list in more detail at a later stage.

Towards the end of what is called 'the British UFO wave of 1967' there occurred a frightening encounter with a weird creature, again in Surrey. As it did not coincide with a UFO sighting it did not at first attract attention, and the writer of the report actually apologizes for including it in a collection of encounter stories. He called it *The Spectre of Winterfold* and speculated that it could have been some kind of 'projected image'. However that may be, it scared a couple of youngsters out of their wits.

On a damp and cloudy night in November 1967, at about 12.30 a.m., *Philip Freeman* and *Angela Carter* left Cranleigh by car, travelling along a twisting, deserted country lane. About two miles from their starting-point Philip left the car, a Triumph Vitesse, to wipe the badly misted-up window, when the couple were unpleasantly surprised by an evil smell as of a stink-bomb. Back in the car, Philip noticed a face pressed up against the side-window. He describes it as rather featureless, but at the same time well defined. In the prevailing gloom of the night it must have been luminous. An arm-like structure touched the top of the hood. Like the Allans he panicked and felt icy cold. Unfortunately the young lady was in an even worse state and in no mood to investigate. Alarmed by the expression on Philip's face, which was one of utter terror, she could only think of getting away. The figure had by now moved to the back and was looking in by the rear window. Its body was bell-shaped. Philip got home in a shock, shaken by what he had seen. It happened in a part of the county noted for sightings of pumas associated with a strong ammoniacal smell. (Strange odours, however, also occur with hauntings, while in time past the Devil enjoyed a reputation for evil odours.)

A reputable French journal dedicated to the study of UFO phenomena recounts the adventures of M. *Cyrus* in August 1975, a no-nonsense middle-aged man of 48. One night we find him in his car near Noé at a quarter to eleven at night. By the light of the moon he fancies that he sees hovering above a field an aluminium-coloured machine about seventy metres in length. At first hardly discernible in the dark sky, it becomes phosphorescent. Presently he notes a dazzling light of the brightness of the sun and M. Cyrus lands in a ditch! He then records a lot of fluctuation in the amount of illumination emitted by the object, which moves without the slightest sound. Another motorist appears on the scene and fears that Cyrus's car has exploded. And indeed its owner was by now in a state of severe shock, doubting whether he was still alive. This then has all the hallmarks of a deliberate attack by a craft which had buzzed him, descending to within 20 cm of the bonnet of his prized Peugeot 404.

It faded gradually to a point of light. This is also very common. People have complained that by the time other witnesses appeared on the scene, or when they got out their camera, there was little left to be seen.

For a long time he was unable to speak; also his watch no longer functioned properly. He became very tired and had trouble with his eyes (another well-known feature). However, in this case the vehicle was all right and there were no landing marks. Once again the supposedly immeasurably superior technology of the extraterrestrials which (accidentally?) causes malfunctions to our own hardware, in this particular instance caused no physical effects, deleterious or otherwise, leaving no tangible proof of its presence as (selectively) elsewhere.

Surprisingly enough, Cyrus was not too astonished

by all this, for it had happened to him before on several occasions! As a 'repeater', apparently genetically or otherwise prone to the UFO experience, he had previously seen an enormous disc that lit up the whole countryside, putting out the lights in a village. The same kind of cause he held responsible for his radio having *played* when switched off.

South America tends to be singled out by whatever orchestrates these mysterious events, the most incredible things being reported from that part of the world. It is commonly stated that these sightings occur in waves in specific areas rather than isolated occurrences. 1965 and 1968 were exceptionally active periods, just as 1974 has been christened the Year of the Ufonauts in the USA. Teleportation, a relatively rare but well-attested feature of psychical research, is mentioned. To make these reports all the more impressive, sightings were often attributable to experienced pilots, sometimes with radar backup.

Not everyone like the artist *Parravicini* saw entities as part of his UFO encounter, but one man is said to have fainted at the mere sight of a 'tall slim being' that did nothing worse than approach him. We are not told why he over-reacted in this way. Generally speaking though, such strange creatures who affect folk very strangely are of special interest since they rule out the usual misperception and illusions inspired by ordinary stimuli.

In *Quilmes* a woman was allegedly forced to enter a craft by an invisible power. She met two men in metallic clothing transmitting light; it shone also from their shoes and helmets. Giants and dwarves feature in such encounters; here the former were in evidence. One was over two meters, another a fraction shorter. She couldn't follow what they were saying, so they did not communicate 'by telepathy' and the heat inside their craft was intolerable. It was round with a small coloured window set in motion by pressing a button. Safely back on earth she found herself near a cemetery.

No doubt there were an awful lot of aliens around in South America at that time. However one is to account for their existence — and plenty of hypotheses vie with each other, ranging from hallucination or holographs to something more sinister — the percipient is often knocked out or otherwise physically affected as if by radiation, with the eyes bulging or swelling immediately after the encounter. A psychogenetic causation cannot be ruled out in view of the power of the mind on the body. (The stigmata are among the most curious of such manifestations.)

Monsieur *Masse*'s unpleasant little men in their tight-fitting greyish-green dresses were like the little green men of the familiar cartoon with pumpkin heads and large slanting eyes, high fleshy cheeks, lipless mouths and pointed chins. They immobilized him with their traditional pencil-shaped 'space-guns'. Whether these comic-book characters really caused the paralysis by 'superior technology', or whether some obscure psychological mechanism was at work, is an open question. They left no trace after their noiseless departure, and it reads like the usual mixture of fantasy and reality which one so often finds in these almost unbelievable accounts. Two leading ufologists, one English, the other French (conversant with the local dialect), were impressed by Masse's sincerity, who sometimes wished that he had kept quiet. It was not the only sighting in that region. Typically, he felt obliged to withhold some of the data, but his integrity is not in doubt. Peter Day also does not tell all; neither do some of the religious visionaries. Strangely, nothing but a few straggling weeds would grow on the landing-site and it had to be ploughed up. One lesson to be learned from this case is that the encounter was not as accidental as Mr. Burtoo's. Masse 'knows' his aliens and is aware of their motivation and always knows when they are around.

In 1972, Mrs *Puddy* a young Australian housewife was driving in her car at some distance from Melbourne, when she noticed a blue light. She took it to be a helicopter, but further inspection revealed it as a low-flying object of enormous size. It was not her only experience of this kind, for in the same month and almost in the same place, she was again struck by that light. Her engine cut out and she lost control of the car. Although it was pitch dark outside, everything was bathed in that blue kind of illumination. She sat still, terrified and unable to move. A glowing object was buzzing her. She perceived no figures, but a voice resounded in her head declaring that 'her test' would prove negative. Another message referred to 'the media' and then told her reassuringly that no harm was intended to her and that she was again in control. Sure enough, the engine started up at this point. The messages, the first of which did not make much sense, were supposed to be 'telepathic' and as if translated. Her experience ran true to type in that everything took place while she was in a car along a desolate stretch of road. Unusual lights in the sky were reported by two independent witnesses.

The *Callery* UFO, with occupants, was seen one night in 1971 by a young couple driving to Pittsburgh. Note that the journey took them along unfrequented roads. They 'assimilated' their sighting to that of an aircraft, but the object, yellow-white and aglow, eventually shot away until it became a mere point of light. We have heard it all before!

In the much-publicized Hill abduction the car was chased by another bright light until it disappeared (it may have been Jupiter). At Callery, the UFO was reduced to a 'small point of light', described as of 'about the brightness of the planet Jupiter'. Presently the object returned and increased in size, shape-shifting into a couple of bowls put together one upon the other at the rims. Its luminescence attracted the woman's attention. It had rectangular and round windows. Visible within them, bathed in a red light, there were two human figures ten feet tall. They terrified the couple when they saw them silhouetted in the upper window. The investigator knows them well; one is *Marion Lang*, the other *Dennis Donaldson*.

Yet another young couple, from *Piedmont* in Italy, were driving home from a party when the husband observed something bright in the sky. Its motions were erratic, but its most notable feature was what they took to be its lit-up cockpit. A detailed description enabled someone to make a drawing of what they saw, the bright lights suggesting the strobe-lights of a police-car. Three human shapes occupied the supposed cockpit of the craft; their large grey rounded helmets were opaque with the kind of exhaling device used by frogmen. This agrees with many other reports of ufonauts dressed up, as it were, in spaceman or frogman outfits as if to suggest that they were unaccustomed to the earth's atmosphere. As there is a marked lack of consistency in this (as in many other respects) we may suspect this piece of 'evidence' as something in the nature of a charade. At any rate, they succeeded in terrorizing the wife, if that was indeed the object of the exercise. As in other cases, there is some supportive evidence of the sighting. Unfortunately the husband did not remember to fetch his camera which was in the house over which the display took place, and now regrets having reported the sighting of the aliens and their space-ship.

Photographs of aliens are invariably suspect and incapable of verification and fairly rare at that.

The *Vilvorde* humanoid sighting perpetuates one of those seemingly ridiculous and apparently meaningless encounters that make this subject so intractable. Vilvorde is an industrial town in Flanders twelve kilometres NE of the capital. The (anonymous) 28-year old witness was indoors in a property adjoining a walled Ursuline convent. It was a cold day in December 1973. He woke and went to the outdoor lavatory. On his way his attention was drawn to a noise and a green light outside that made him glance through the kitchen window. There he was surprised to see a small creature in a one-piece garment emitting green light. The little man wore the traditional helmet. Attached at the back was some kind of receptacle. The garment worn was seamless and in one piece with a belt. He had a square 'torch' giving out a red light. He wore baggy trousers and small tight boots. A luminous aura or halo surrounded him. He worked in complete silence, although his observer had at first reckoned that he had heard a sound as of a shovel striking the ground.

The illumination as described is equally puzzling: the green light of his clothing in contrast to the red from a box, plus the (unspecified) hue of the halo that illuminated part of the ground and the wall. Everything points to a dream-like scenario with its consequent inconsistencies and illogicalities. The pretence of a scientific exploration in a small backyard of an obscure Belgian town was supported by the use of a 'detector' looking more like a carpet-sweeper! It was being passed over some refuse that was lying there. As if unused to earthly conditions (like the humanoids of Piedmont) the creature moved about stiffly and with difficulty, and even unable to turn his head. The man faced him when he flashed his torch at the entity. He saw a dark face singularly devoid of features apart from a pair of pointed ears. The eyes were well-defined but masked by moving membranes. The strange intruder gave a sign of acknowledgement with his hand and turned towards the wall, ascending it haltingly.

All of a sudden he entered the transparent dome of a round UFO rising vertically, disappearing within the space of a few seconds. There were no unpleasant repercussions, and the Belgian had a snack without bothering his wife and a cousin who was staying with him! Apparently he was as unaffected by what he had just seen as Mr Burtoo, who surprised everyone by getting on with the job of angling without being unduly perturbed by phantoms. There were no physical traces of the visit and no one in the neighbourhood had noticed anything unusual in the night. He, again, was a 'repeater', suggesting that the experience was person-related with a strongly subjective element. But was it just a dream? Many of the details reported by the man are found in the previously-published French translation of an American publication, but he said that he only read it *afterwards*. Again, it does not exhaust all his detailed descriptions of the supposed encounter which we have merely summarized.

No one has as yet come up with a convincing explanation why there are no reports of abductions and close encounters from a large country like Germany or Russia whereas a small one like Belgium can boast of several.

Another from 1974 involves 31 year old *Monsieur X*. One night at about 8.40 he was approaching Warneton on the France-Belgian border when his car-lights went out and his car stopped dead. At a guessed distance of 150 m. he saw what he thought was a load of hay. This object, partly orange and partly white, was found to be supported by three legs. On closer acquaintance it looked more like a helmet. In another typical bout of misperception the Belgian identified two figures as farmers.

This shows that victims of encounters are not as often assumed ignorant and superstitious peasants who see a ghost in every bush and tree in the dark, but rational human beings taken by surprise by something unfamiliar and unbelievable. With him still sitting in the car, the 'farmers' approached him in the customary rigid and deliberate manner of ufonauts. The smaller of the two recalled the Michelin Man of French advertisements. His round helmet had a large window, while in his hand he held the obligatory 'space-gun', pointing it ominously at the car. The second entity's face presented no problem to recognition and was clearly visible since his cube-shaped helmet was opaque at the sides. Basically, both faces were identical, even if quite unlifelike, the heads being pear-shaped and greyish. Their appearance of unreality was enhanced by eyes like marbles with the merest suggestion of eyebrows, a tiny nose, and only a slight indication of a mouth, that contained neither a tongue nor teeth. This perfunctory image of the facial features is in line with general observations of 'ET' entities. Under their chin a black rectangular box was fixed. Their uniform was the standard garb of a dull, grey metallic overall that extended from the finger-tips to the feet. The second figure seemed to be the more athletic of the two. Both had unnaturally long arms.

The witness felt a slight shock. A low-pitched sound grew louder all the time. What makes one think in terms of an apparition was the fact that an attempt to speak proved unsuccessful; for whereas ufonauts are supposed to communicate by telepathy (or are just plainly unintelligible), ghosts are remarkably taciturn and often cannot speak at all. Not content with this, there appeared a third configuration who acted as a kind of immobile sentry or guard. Ufonauts come in twos and threes, and in this important respect differ from ghosts.

The encounter was abruptly concluded when the two original monsters turned in unison, marching briskly towards the waiting space-ship, apparently unaffected by the wet and sticky nature of the terrain. Gone now for good was the common pretence of not being able to move at ease.

After the craft's departure in the usual fantastic way at the speed of lightning, Monsieur X began to wonder whether the whole thing had not been a dream or a hallucination. If the latter, it was apparently verified, to judge by the remark attributed to a motorist who came across him slumped at the wheel in a state of shock. On the other hand, none of the neighbours had noticed anything out of the ordinary. Some support is gained by the fact that both the car-radio and the cassette suffered by the encounter.

It can hardly have been a coincidence that five months later there was an almost exact repeat performance at the same place. This time it was a light summer's night. He was visited by the same two characters who stood by the wayside as if soliciting a lift from a chance passing motorist — who happened to be Monsieur X! There was more mechanical interference, but he stopped the car and remained inside until, a couple of minutes or so later, the entities simply dematerialized and there was no more trouble. Meanwhile he had been overtaken by another car, but its driver seemed not to have noticed anything untoward. This suggests a private experience in which outsiders could not share — another point of contact with the paranormal which has frequently been noted in UFO cases. This second encounter with alien intelligences did not visibly involve 'flying saucers'.

The investigator of this incident remarks that 'the Warneton region has been the scene of happenings that are out of the ordinary, and . . . outside the scope of our normal conception'; a commendably cautious assessment. But how are we to account for all this? As in similar cases, the physical effects expressed in mechanical interference militate against an interpretation on purely psychological terms.

The report of what is known as the case of the *Little Electrical Man* takes us once more to the USA of 1973. It has even stronger psychic overtones, which is hardly surprising in view of the fact that UFO experiences basically seem to belong to the same genre: this being was nearly *transparent*. The subjects were a young couple who lived in a caravan near Albany, Ohio. One October evening the girl was returning home to be confronted by something like 'a person with a close-fitting sheet draped over [its body]', but only four feet tall and rather indistinct. Its stare frightened her. She also refers to a 'bright white light' that gradually disappeared in the adjoining fields. Still in her car, she 'sensed' a strong 'presence'. This ghost-like figure then changed into a kind of electric man used as an advertisement in the States, 2½ feet in height, with an ill-defined face and stumpy arms, but legless. She felt it to be quite friendly and even a little timid, a kind of 'energy form'. There was a rather mechanical look about it, but it stll gave her the impression of being looked at, and she felt ill at ease as a consequence of this sensation. She considered the wider implications of her encounter with an allegedly ET presence and its aim and purpose. Her friend in the caravan had also observed something in the sky.

During the last century Mendoza in the Argentine had been the scene of earthquake-related lights. More recently they were associated with mere tremors. Some researchers now think there is a definite connection between seismic disturbances and UFO sightings and rather wide-sweeping claims have been made. A 1968 case from that region involves two casino workers who went to a hospital complaining that their car had been mysteriously stopped. Five small humanoids had emerged from a saucer and take blood-samples from their fingers, placed some graffiti on the car and vanished.

Juan and Fernando, both in their twenties, were driving home from work when the car suddenly stopped and the lights went out. Both were paralysed. There were no less than five ufonauts on duty. An enormous circular UFO was floating close to the ground, projecting a strong beam of light. It was noted that the aliens were ordinary looking except for their outsize heads, a not uncommon feature. They were bald, clothed in overalls and spoke in an electronic sounding voice, telling the men not to be afraid. Apart from reassuring them, they were treated to the usual trivial nonsense kind of message. If the whole narrative may be thought to tell us nothing new, their story was even retracted by them. Unfortunately the inscriptions incised on the body of the car are meaningless squiggles. In their favour, it is said that when seen on TV the men made a good impression, while the authorities tried to denigrate them. The case is a well-investigated one, but its significance and evaluation are a different matter.

It was common knowledge in days of old that those abducted by the fairies were ill-advised to partake of their food. The Church regarded the latter as in league with the Devil, and a meal was the basic feature of the worship of Satan by his devotees, the witches. In neither case was salt one of the ingredients: the orthodox regarded it as a cleansing agent that did not commend itself to the ungodly. The actual repast was unappetising and moreover served up by demons. Vallee has drawn many parallels between folklore and ufology, and in the following French case the aliens try to force-feed their reluctant victim.

Early one morning a man rode his moped on his way

to work. He did not believe in UFOs but was depressed as the result of what happened to him, the more so as he became the target of ridicule by his work-mates. As a result, he proved an elusive prey for the researchers who found him in a state of total disorientation. His story was that, crossing a bridge over a river, his moped stopped of its own accord and he met what he described as a couple of 'astronauts'. There also lurked in the background something large and dark which he identified as their 'machine'. If he was right in his attribution, it was at any rate unlit and noiseless. This took place on a dark night towards the end of the month of February 1974. When the aliens seized the handlebars he became very scared. One of them then indicated that he wished him to eat something produced out of a pocket or bag. It looked like a piece of chocolate except that it was rather tasteless. The ways of the ETs are as inscrutable as those of the Almighty, since it appeared that the sole point of the episode was to persuade the poor chap to eat this undefinable substance, for as soon as he had done so they took their leave. He was not by nature a curious man, and in his haste to make his escape did not bother to look found.

Here again there are physical traces. The aliens measured about 1.70 m, and affected the traditional ET guise (or disguise) which he seems to have been ready to accept in spite of his original scepticism because of their appropriate accoutrement. Their helmets were unusually *square-shaped*. He failed to recognize any features through the opening of the helmet. Their separate long gloves were 'like the gloves worn for the artificial insemination of cattle'.

In view of the genetic engineering experiments recently attributed to some ufonauts, this observation is of more than passing interest, going back as it does 16 years.

Do humanoids relish human nourishment which, as

we are told every day by some nutritional expert or other, may expose us to the dangers of various diseases? There is at present no clear answer, but food does enter into some other ufological accounts as well. The best known comes from America and is called the Eagle River case of *Joe Simonton* and the pancakes. The story goes that Simonton, a chicken-farmer in Wisconsin, was presented with three cakes cooked on board a UFO.

He was not impressed as the one he ate tasted 'like cardboard', and the scientific analysis carried out by the American Air Force found no unusual or unearthly ingredients. It was an ordinary pancake! Simonton saw his UFO on an April morning in 1961. It was bright and silvery and hovered above the ground. Its dimensions were 12 x 30 feet. There were three humanoids inside who are fairly minutely described. Their general appearance was 'Italian'. They measured 5', had dark hair and skin. One was dressed in black, two with knit helmets above turtle-neck tops. One indicated that he wanted water and produced a jug which Simonton obligingly filled. Returning from his house he noticed that some sort of frying was going on inside the craft; at the same time he heard the hum of a generator. The whole scene was rendered even more realistic (or superficially plausible) by the presence of instrument panels. As he showed interest in the cooking, he was handed three of the pancakes which had holes within a diameter of three inches. When the hatch of the UFO was finally closed it was almost as if all of one piece. It departed with a tremendous blast bending the trees. There was no physical proof of its presence and in view of the experient's good reputation, the episode was put down to a dream. Still, there were the pancakes!

The next episode, this time nearer home, is bizarre in the extreme. It is known as the case of the 'Mince-Pie Martians'. It is justifiably described as 'one of the strangest, if not most absurd, UFO-related events ever.' It first appeared in the *Flying Saucer Review*, was well investigated, and its physical effects are more than usually impressive both in their range and in their extent. The percipient (now deceased) had a clear memory of the alleged events which thus did not require hypnotic recall. Early one morning in January 1979 she waved her husband good-bye as he left for work. *Jean Hingley* lived modestly at Rowley Regis near Birmingham. Outside it was exceptionally cold and had been snowing. Suddenly she was surprised to see 'a large orange sphere' over the roof of the car-port. Whatever it was radiated heat and turned white as it came nearer to hover over the back garden. Her dog became paralysed with fear and froze 'like a statue', his hackles were up, and his eyes were fixed on the mysterious sight. Suddenly three small figures rushed into her house as if carried by a current of wind. She felt cold, drained and very weak.

Back in her living-room Jean was amazed to be confronted by two fairy-like entities that were attacking her Christmas tree. On the top of the tree was a 'fairy' which they managed to dislodge. The ufonauts were very much like the latter, but larger. They were 3½ feet tall and enclosed in a silvery kind of tunic adorned with six frontal silver buttons. They had large black lustrous eyes in an otherwise almost featureless white face that was covered by a transparent helmet like a goldfish bowl — a rather ludicrous version of the diver's outfit known from other cases. The helmets were crowned by a small lamp. They sported silver-green limbs minus hands or feet. These rather lifeless puppets had big wings that were oval and looked artificial as if made of paper, so thin as to be transparent and covered with bright dots. These kitsch creatures were luminous with thin streamers hanging down from them.

For a whole hour Jean watched awestruck as these

unlikely creatures flew around her room as if mechanical and lacking any indication of real, biological life. Their arms were held in a fixed position, their legs hung stiffly, their faces betrayed no emotion or expression. Jean meanwhile was paralysed; her mouth wide open, her eyes staring. She could not even turn her head to look for a third fairy which had found its way into her house. The physiological effect did not wear off immediately after the return to normality. There were slight attempts at conversation, but at a very infantile level of intelligence: perhaps it was unreasonable to expect too much by the way of education or superior artistic taste of either party to the encounter. An effect basically similar to that of the traditional 'space-gun' was observed coming from the helmets of the entities. Jean was dazzled and even blinded, and suffered a burning sensation where she was hit by a beam. Although the meeting was unpleasant for the experient, she was reassured by the aliens that no harm was meant to her.

Do ufonauts eat and drink as we do? Jean (who really had no particular reason to humour these unwelcome intruders) asked them whether they would care for a drink. They answered in unison, saying, 'water, water, water'. Jean offered them four glasses of water, one for herself and a plate of mince-pies! Although she was unable to see them drink, because she had again been blinded, the presumption is that the water had been actually drunk as the glasses were afterwards found to be empty. (In the case of a doctor's relative two Men In Black accepted drinks at dinner but did not touch them. Maria's drank hot coffee but still had hands that felt like icicles.)

As to the more solid refreshment offered, it is uncertain how they reacted to it in the long run. Each one is said to have 'lifted' a mince-pie, but again they were not seen to eat. Jean had some other left-overs from the recent festivities: cigars and cigarettes, but these were refused. Perhaps they did not know what to do with them? Jean thought she had to show them how to smoke — although some may not consider it a necessary accomplishment for child-like robots. Their reaction was unexpected. On the point of lighting up, a deafening noise was heard from the garden area where the UFO had landed, though Jean was not aware of this fact. She concluded, presumably correctly, that her strange visitors were afraid of fire. However that may have been, they just 'shot back' in apparent alarm.

Meanwhile the noise increased to a high pitch and Jean for the first time caught sight of a 'space-ship' glowing orange, 18 x 4 feet. Its port-holes were aglow. Its surface was of shining plastic with a funny sort of aerial, crowned with something rather like a chimney-sweep's brush. The entities now simply 'glided out', not using their wings, which did not seem to serve any particular purpose. They appear to have possessed some kind of translation device. It was apparently connected to buttons on their chests which they kept on pressing, making painful bleeping sounds. On departing, they were still holding the mince-pies. Once back in their craft after this encounter with a human being, the door closed by sliding to and (as usual) no trace of an opening could be detected. The woman was in agony as the result of her experience.

The UFO left an apparent trace in the snow and for a year the grass would not grow in that part of her garden. There were a number of other unexplained physical effect attributed to the landing, such as the malfunctioning of the TV set, the stopping of her clock, the ruin of the radio and the cassette-tapes. Also, her gold wedding-ring turned white on the outside. She was so badly affected that she had to take time off work. Her Christmas tree disappeared only to return in pieces. Jean

Hingley comes over as an intelligent woman highly thought of by everyone, though with only a basic education. The case is currently still under investigation by BUFORA researcher Albert Budden.

Equally debatable is the information about ET consumption of food and drink in a recent report. The report deals with a *retired major* who lived in a remote part of Sussex. He claims to have been repeatedly visited by entities of a frail and withered appearance who fail to articulate properly. They were offered fruit and whiskey. It appears that they disliked the latter, but it is not known whether they liked the fruit; the implication being that they ate it. In return they presented him with some 'uncut diamonds' that turned out to be worthless bits of quartz. Mrs. *Andreason* (an abductee) was given a 'small book', but it disappeared at one point, though her daughter remembered it.

Unfortunately the hard evidence given to humans by the aliens always turns out to be inconclusive and where furtive abductees had tried to steal items they did not get away with it. An *Argentinian* boy abductee was presented with a glove which was subsequently snatched away, while *Helen White* was deceived into thinking that she would obtain important proof. We have to rely on unsupported evidence of a single witness in most cases of alien communication. (In cases where the Virgin is seen the witness is sometimes given 'proof' which is sometimes is in the form of a temporary loss of senses or ability such as going dumb or losing the sense of hearing.

There a few accounts of Finnish humanoids, but one is on record. One afternoon twenty years ago a *forester* and a *farmer* were skiing in a forest in Southern Finland. At sunset they rested in the icy, inhospitable countryside, when they were surprised by a buzzing sound coming from a powerful light in the sky. This one was remarkable in that it was part of a luminous cloud containing a metallic-looking object about three meters in diameter. It gradually descended until it almost reached the ground. The rather constant feature of a bright beam was followed by a mist and the forester felt as if he had been attacked from behind. Gradually he became aware of a presence, within the beam, holding a box emitting a yellow pulsating light. The creature was only 90 cm high with spindly arms and legs and, at the centre of the face, which was pale and waxen, there was what looked like a hook! The ears were tiny. This unappealing creature wore a light green overall and was shod in long dark green boots. It was holding a box in clawlike fingers. Both men saw this monstrosity, straight out of a children's comic but, again, not too unlike one of the 'Little Folk' from the Old Country.

The farmer describes a luminous and phosphorescent configuration with thin, slanting shoulders and the arms of a child, but did not notice anything about the clothes except their green colour; one of the exceptional *real* 'little green men' so beloved of the media! He mentioned a conical metallic helmet.

It will be seen that the two independent descriptions do not totally tally. Celia Green in her study of apparitions makes the point that this is often true of collectively perceived ghosts and quotes an amusing case in which the dominant percipient rebukes another for an allegedly incorrect view of what must be presumed to have been, technically speaking, some kind of hallucination.

The blinding lights from the magic box were meanwhile directed towards the forester. The mist began to thicken, as a result of which the alien (unusually on his own) became invisible. The experience seemed to end without causing too much trepidation. Notwithstanding this, it affected the forester physically. He collapsed and for several months suffered from symptoms like headaches and bouts of vomiting. He protested about his government's failure to support him during his illness. His friend was more fortunate in only being affected to a minor extent. Severe radiation effects were complained of as they were in a similar sighting by two American women who also were not compensated by the authorities who claimed to be uninvolved.

The two men in the present case are known to be of good character and unlikely to have perpetrated a hoax or to have made false claims. But neither was the creature a plausible denizen of Outer Space.

The *Greensburg* episode is exceptionally important in having been investigated by B.E. Schwartz, the noted American psychiatrist and researcher into the paranormal. The location is a farm near Greensburg, U.S.A. A farmer, Stephen, in the company of many others had in October 1973, at about 9 p.m., been struck by the sight of a 'bright red ball' hovering over a field. It turned white, lighting up the whole area. Someone had fancied that he had seen a couple of bears and fired off a rifle. There was something very strange about the creatures which measured 7 and 8 feet respectively. Hairy, they sported greenish-yellow eyes, with arms nearly touching the ground. They cried out like babies, but reeked of burning rubber. Hit by several bullets, they just took refuge in the woods, apparently none the worse for being shot at. In this respect they parallel the monkey-like apparitions at Kelly which also proved impervious to close-range attacks with gunfire. Some of the observers' eyes started to smart and it was noticed that the farm animals kept out of range. When the Police arrived on the scene they were apprehensive of something in the woods being capable of giving a kind of glow.

One of the young men, Stephen went berserk. Dr Schwartz diagnosed that such behaviour for Stephen was completely out of character. Dr. Schwartz believed that it was 'a specific reaction to the UFO-creature experience and the trauma and terror . . . nearly unhinged Stephen'. It was evidently one of those monsters which even in these enlightened days are still occasionally observed; or again not unlike a werewolf, or a case of lycanthropy (man into animal).

CHAPTER SIX

Mind Monsters: Invaders from Inner Space is the title of a recent study by Jenny Randles, Britain's leading ufologist. It deals with a diversity of related topics, including UFOs. Among these pride of place could be given to the study of the Incubus/Succubus syndrome, prominent in the post-medieval period and erroneously thought to be a thing of the past.

Demonologists of the Renaissance subtly distinguished the male incubus from his female counterpart (the succubus). The former derives etymologically from *incubare* (Latin for 'to lie on') while the latter comes from *succubare* ('to lie under').

Close encounters — especially the variety known as 'bedroom invaders' are often an *indoor* phenomenon associated with sleep, or with those intermediate states when you are about to fall asleep or on the point of waking up. They are known in psychology as 'hypnagogic' and 'hypnopompic'. It is believed that these states are particularly conducive to seeing apparitions and entities.

Randles quotes a Canadian example of a young man waking up in the middle of the night in a state of total paralysis. Two diminutive figures appeared at the foot of his bed. Outsiders confirmed that there had been a bluish glow in the sky, rising slowly. MacKenzie chronicles many accounts of 'bedroom invaders' of a psychic kind: if there was any UFO involvement, it was not recorded.

While some may talk of nightmares, this is inappropriate in this context as implying sleep. The experiences are almost always described as involving full consciousness of surroundings and, for instance, a light is seen to be shinging through a door. Prof Hufford in his recent study of *The Terror that comes in the Night* explains that 'The victims are awake and . . . hear and see and feel odd-sounding things.'

Confusion has also been created by psychoanalytical misinterpretation. Hufford established 'at least three types of nocturnal experiences ; a variety of dreams, sexual encounters with 'supernaturals' . . . and attacks . . . without any sexuality.' What Hufford calls the 'Old Hag'-type of attack is described in the following typical example which is of special interest because of its alleged UFO connection.

The sighting commenced with the appearance of a 'light across the Bay' in Canada. '*John*', the experient, regarded this preliminary episode with ill-deserved contempt. His account, however, includes 'all four of the primary Old Hag features'. These embrace being awake, immobility with some possible sensation of pressure, plus normal perception of the surroundings. Paranormal footsteps (a standard feature of haunted houses) are interwoven into the narrative. A luminous figure meanwhile glowed ominously in the dark.

We shall continue with our effort of setting the phenomena within their historical context, confident that light can thus be thrown on an enigma. By 1100 AD Christian dogma concerning the gross double-act of demonic molestation was 'solidly established as an article of learned faith throughout Western Europe'. A recent study has established similar occurrences on a solidly investigated foundation as still (or again?) flourishing in Newfoundland and elsewhere. Alleged violations of the human body by obscure, sinister entities is not uncommon; not necessarily in connection with black magic, but spontaneously. Says Hufford by way of caution, 'The precise distinctions which were made . . . between voluptuous sleep-related experiences and attacks of the Old Hag type are difficult to determine.'

We have already recounted Cotton Mather's account of paralysis and fear induced through a spectral visitation to one Richard Coman, in which an occult agency working through a New England witch took the rap. This nocturnal attack is an above-average example of 'spectral evidence' produced in court in the 17th century.

Persona, in the 14th century, knew of an unusual incubus-like creature flourishing in Germany in the household of a certain 'renowned knight' attracted by his beautiful sister. Numerous as were its alleged accomplishments, they did not include visibility. 'Slender and soft' hands were, however, part and parcel of this configuration and it is relevant to reflect on the little-known fact that 'spirit hands', detached from the body, are amply attested in the mediumistic literature of the 19th and early 20th centuries.

If we can believe Guazzo, females enslaved by the Power of Darkness were rewarded with an incubus in the form of a 'rank goat' — an animal at that time most unjustly despised. Caietano, another writer on witchcraft, tells of 'a woman in love whom the devil anointed naked, promising that he would take her to her lover.' In an unconscious, or altered, state of consciousness she actually imagined that she was with him, but it was only a delusion. Similarly, some scholars think that when people report that they have been transported into UFOs and meet alien creatures from Outer Space they are merely fantasising; but whether or not there is any satanic involvement in such fancies is of course another matter.

According to Johann Meyfarth (1635) not only hundreds of women, but (as he reluctantly admits) even *men*, confessed to having had sex with demons. Such departures from acceptable behaviour were dismissed as illusions by Thummius. The full relevance of this needs to be considered together with the revelations of Hopkins and Strieber. At one time all this was taken seriously; but by the reign of Louis XV of France it was considered to be a huge joke. The Incubus and his ilk were now at best relegated to the realm of imagination, leading the way to ultimate misinterpretation of the phenomenon. Still, it had its use as an alibi: 'To conceal sin, a woman, a girl, a nun in name only, a debauchee, who affects the appearance of virtue, will palm off her lover for an incubus spirit which haunts her.'

As a cloak for immorality it served Bishop Sylvanus, whose physical form was assumed by a certain Sister's incubus — undeterred naturally by the then still distant prospect of the jibes of the Elizabethan Reginald Scot and, no doubt, of other unsung and more contemporary puritanical sceptics.

In a similar vein is Sinistrari's moral tale about the religious woman who locked herself in after dinner. An ever-inquisitive Sister bored a hole through the wall of her cell, when all was revealed: an all-too-earthly lover was masquerading as a Spirit! On the other hand, what are we to think of him who sang 'the most dirty songs' in which his modest virgin victim refused to join? Surely, that one was a demon of the lower regions! For once there is a happy ending to her endurance, for the young lady's earnest prayers, supplications and tears drove away whatever it was, and thus Margaret of Cortena was left in peace to her meditations.

When it comes to the sex act, there is a lack of

consensus of learned opinion among the prelates of the Church, who had not as yet learned to confine their attention to matters purely political. Some were satisfied that it gave full gratification to the demons themselves, but this is not the considered opinion of St Thomas Aquinas, the supreme authority on all matters pertaining to witchcraft and demonology.

A similar unresolved dilemma relates to the victims of lewd demonic attention. At times it appears as almost rapturous, but at others the reverse. Scot quotes Nider to the effect that 'Heretofore ... *Incubus* was fain to ravish women against their will'; however around 1400 AD there occurred an (unexplained) change of attitude, so that now 'Witches consent willingly to their desire.'

If Nider was right, and morals were no longer up to their former lofty standards after that critical date, it is strange that there are nowadays once more so many reported cases of forced intercourse with non-human entities. Meanwhile Nider appears to gain support from reports such as that of the seventeenth century maiden who, pursued by a demon 'seemed almost afraid of being delivered from the devil.' And worse to come: a nubile German sorceress was so depraved that she would actually *summon* her incubus!

The long and wearisome catalogue, compiled by monks, of crimes attributed to the witches who, like present day contactees, may have been just more psychically receptive, includes ligature to cause impotence among a man and his wife. Christian Stridbeck, in his treatise *Van den Hexen (Concerning Witches*; 1723) describes the different ways of achieving this object; some apparently too indelicate to narrate. It is, at any rate, not specially pertinent to the subject of ufology, where the aliens are represented as more intent on interbreeding than on causing mere mischief, however unpleasant may be the side-effects of their contact with us.

The phenomenology of the paranormal has an uncanny way of adapting to novel developments in culture and philosophy and of fooling us in the process. Those who study the copious data of folklore, psychical research (parapsychology) and ufology in isolation and without any attempt at cross-reference, deprive themselves effectively of all hope of obtaining any profound measure of understanding of the underlying causes of these strange and often almost impenetrable anomalies. None is more obscure and inscrutable than the Incubus/Succubus syndrome and — in the update of the day — the survival of the 'legend' of the Old Hag, taken along with the more unpalatable aspects of UFO abductions, which retain all the vitality as well as the mystery of ancient occult lore as specified in witchcraft and the cult of the fairies.

A recent, and less extreme, example is what happened to *Elsa*, a young Englishwoman. A number of years ago she was living in a hostel in London. One night in 1973 she awoke to find a girl 'pacing up and down'. A light was shining through the door of the hall. Elsa was very scared, especially when the figure lifted up the cover of her bed to get in with her. In the written report she expands, 'I then saw the body bearing down on me and at the same time my head crashed back on the pillow very quickly as if it had been pushed. I heard a loud cracking sound as if my head hit the pillow and I was unconscious'. (Elsa suggested incidentally that there had been the usual escalation of hypothesis; she originally thought that the figure was a German girl who — she then remembered — was no longer at the hostel).

Similar accounts are numerous, and American parapsychologist Scott Rogo cites a recent case of psychological orientation in which he stresses the 'sexual influence' exerted on a middle-aged man by a nocturnal apparition in which he detects overtones of guilt and frustration.

The phenomenon is familiar to the Chinese, who call it 'being pressed by a ghost'. Charles Emmons in his study of *Chinese Ghosts and ESP* quotes a case in which 'a short, fat . . . woman in her thirties floated into the room like the wind, came up to my bed and lay on top of me, face down, looking at me.' (The author puts this experience down to sleep paralysis and lowered blood pressure.)

In a recent book by veteran ghost-hunter Andrew MacKenzie, he recounts under the general heading of 'Something Under the Bed', how a fellow Council member of the SPR encountered a 'bed-room invader' at 3 o'clock in the morning. *Dr Dewsbury*, a psychiatrist, was 'violently roused by the mattress being pushed from underneath as if by someone under the bed.' As usual, there was nothing to account for the disturbance, any more than for the rocking motion complained of to Hufford, or for what Kittredge has christened the 'bedclothes trick', when the covers are pulled off the unwary and drowsy sleeper — whether by goblins or by the, marginally more respectable, poltergeist.

MacKenzie once more discusses the phenomenon of 'a stranger in the bed' and the location is the French capital. Mme *Bourget* and her husband were staying at the time in a Paris hotel. Suddenly she awoke to the 'impression of being between two persons.' Oppressed by a feeling of evil, she refused to dismiss this sensation as a mere nightmare. Mrs *Hellstroem* of the Swedish Society for Psychical Research fared no better. Two successive nocturnal phantoms invaded the privacy of a large double-bed. But, as Jenny Randles points out in *Mind Monsters*, such uninvited visitors are not invariably considered evil, though often unwelcome. Years after her encounter with aliens and a UFO, my friend from Wales, now happily married, is still harassed at night. Randles has been contacted by a youth who wakes up in the middle of the night and claims such experiences as being paralysed and drained. A young woman from North London saw a tall male figure materialise out of a blue light when she was only thirteen.

Another girl, *Rachel*, is disconcerted by waking up from all too realistic dreams, paralysed and dizzy, to be confronted by an ugly diminutive entity which even frightened her dog. Randles thinks it possible that she either moulds or perceives 'amorphous and ambiguous shapes' which are basically mere 'malleable gasses.'

In view of all these data, some taking us back to remote periods of time, it is obvious that prejudice often too hastily dismisses ancient records as worthless superstition of credulous folk engulfed in an aura of unreason when Man's critical faculties were as yet insufficiently evolved; our grounds to pause are all the more founded when we realize that in one form or another such beliefs reflect a possible basic mental structure that has survived the shock of the intellectual revision of cultural change — in spite of modern obsession with technology and undoubted great advances in psychological reinterpretation.

Hilary Evans, who has done more than anyone else in recent times to explore such enigmas, has suggested that UFO reports may be as insubstantial as those of witchcraft. Before this conclusion becomes consolidated and incorporated into the consensus of informed opinion, it will have to be proved that all that goes under the name of Black Magic can be adequately dismissed as 'a plausible fantasy created by the Church . . . and accepted by the common people' being in fact (as argued by Evans) nothing more than 'a combination of social and psychological forces.' This may be an oversimplification, both being expressions of the same basic phenomenon.

Fashions change, and not only in clothes, though Evans is right in claiming that the Emperor's delusion may persist. At one time it was assumed with confidence that the enlightenment of the Reformation had done away with 'figments of the imagination' like apparitions and few people nowadays believe that disarranged beds prove the activities of mischievous goblins, seeing that goblins are no longer in vogue. By contrast, not everyone laughs at the concept of entities hailing from ever-expanding distances in Outer Space in preposterous machines with nothing better in mind than to impregnate earthlings for reasons best known to themselves, and incidentally to mock us by imitating our probes on the moon and to indulge in nonsense talk as if they were retarded children while they present themselves in the guise corresponding to an assumed advanced state of more fashionable science than, say, the biblical giants of old who came in pursuit of the Daughters of Man.

Meanwhile we have to admit that we are faced with mysteries beyond our powers of comprehension, but on which psychology and its more recent parameter, parapsychology, can throw light. It is in this direction that we must look for enlightenment. For the present though, being like Squire Scot 'wearied with so many lecheries most horrible and very filthy and fabulous actions and passions..together with spirit *Incubus*', we must turn again to the detailed examination of further modern cases of encounters and abduction.

CHAPTER SEVEN

In Brazil, a soldier arrived in an exhausted condition at a railway station, acting (so it was thought) suspiciously. The extraordinary story that transpired was that the soldier, *Jose Antonio da Silva*, had taken a fishing holiday in the spring of 1969. The trip proved a disappointment as he caught nothing. Disappointment was to give way to dismay and terror when, on the Sunday afternoon of his trip, he was assaulted by a hidden force by the lake, dragged through the swamp by two or three masked creatures, all apparently armed. It seemed to him that they had fired at his legs. This deed of unprovoked aggression came from humanoids no more that 1.20 m in height in strange light-coloured shining garments. They wore aluminium coloured masks with small holes for the eyes; these were connected to plastic tubes leading to metal containers which they carried on their backs. Whether Jose was aware of it or not, his kidnappers were of the familiar diver or astronaut make-belief type.

He then saw something which resembled 'a water tumbler with its base set on a saucer and with a large saucer, upside down, placed on top of its mouth.'

Jose was taken inside into a room made of stone, an unlikely building material for the interior walls of a space-craft! Blinding light shone without any obvious source. This is a common feature in these reports. He was made to wear a helmet with attachments in the shape of tubes and everyone was secured for take-off. The general impression gained by the soldier was that the arrangements were elementary and far from superior technology. But then, of course, the whole thing was one big sham; a gigantic hoax perpetrated on the unsuspecting Jose; but by whom and why? This total lack of plausibility, and indeed realism, was increased by his captors' lack of proper articulation in deep guttural sounds which meant nothing to him. The whole scenario recalls apparitions that effect a certain amount of realism of presentation but stop short of being totally convincing because they cannot speak or have the greatest difficulty in saying even a few words; yet ufonauts are voluble enough when it comes to delivering 'messages'.

Jose felt uncomfortable because of the primitive conditions aboard the 'space-ship'. With relief he noted that it had finally landed. The humanoid occupants, though small, were very strong for their size and carried him by his armpits, having first blindfolded him. All of a sudden they became quiet, whereas they had previously been talkative, even if impossible to understand. There were in addition to theirs a lot of other voices. Taken to another room, he was confronted by a taller figure which he took to be that of their chief; this was after the blindfold had been removed. Strangely, this person apparently required neither space-suit nor helmet. His long hair was matched by his outsize beard. Even his eyebrows gave the impression of being abnormally thick. His pale large green eyes scarcely blinked as he studied his captive with evident, but hardly reciprocated, satisfaction. The presumed boss was as quaint as any such creature on record. His nose and ears were out of proportion and too large and his wide toothless mouth gave him a fish-like appearance.

Jose, however, was now more at ease as his captor was of a pleasant demeanour. Presently he was to be joined by up to a dozen similar entities. If there was an door through which they had come it was not obvious as Jose's helmet made it hard for him to see. He felt alarmed when he saw what appeared to be human corpses on a shelf. They were naked with closed eyes. A close inspection of his property was to follow. It had been bundled up and consisted of his angling equipment plus a few other items; among it they retained his identity card. The ufonauts were armed with what seemed like ray guns that produced a luminous beam.

Using sketches their leader indicated to Jose that he wanted to take Jose's possessions, perhaps assuming that they were the equivalent of ray guns. Jose did not agree to this request. Other subjects that formed part of the discussion between them are not described. He was made to drink from a stone cup. The contents were bitter to the taste. Jose says he was asked to act as an informant, but he did not agree to this request much to the annoyance of his captors.

Soon everything was interrupted by the appearance of a human-like person who appeared to be a holy man dressed like a friar. Jose now received a comforting revelation of a characteristically furtive type.

Eventually, after further adventures in space-travel, he found himself in unfamiliar surroundings, hungry and thirsty. He discovered that he was far from home, and had been away for four and a half days. He had difficulties in walking and was worried about the loss of his identity-card which had been taken by the aliens who unfortunately did not leave any object which would establish their own identity.

Intensive research showed that Jose Antonio was a man of good reputation and a pious Catholic. The physical symptoms complained of by him (particularly the trouble with his eyes) gradually disappeared as was to be expected, but he continued to be worried about the drink that had been forced upon him, in case it had given his captors power over him — a touch that recalls folklore beliefs. (Refreshments offered by fairies or witches are to be shunned at all cost.) Indeed, he has since been visited by three entities in his garden, all in their uniforms. It made him apprehensive about their motives and, at a higher level, even more so about the future of mankind.

Can such cases be accepted at face-value? Jose had no witnesses to his experience which, to him at least, must have been real enough and whose psychological effect can not be underestimated. But what is its message? Most people's boggle-threshold is vastly exceeded by the chronicling of such marvels, but it is unwise to ignore such reports.

This also applies to our next case from Africa. *Geller*, according to his biographer, has had encounters with UFOs and was even teleported in a car. In URI by Andrija Puharich (published in 1947) the author details this teleportation which was received with scepticism as nothing of the kind had then been heard of. This next account from Southern Rhodesia (Zimbabwe) has been described as possibly 'one of the most important' reports of supposed UFO activity and is certainly one of the most sensational.

During the last days of May in 1974, a young couple, *Peter and Frances*, were motoring from Salisbury, Southern Rhodesia, to Durban, South Africa. Peter had been speeding, and was afraid of being caught by a speed-trap, when the couple noted the presence by the roadside of what they took to be a policeman holding a walkie-talkie. They were however slightly disconcerted by a certain discrepancy: the man was wearing a metallic-looking suit instead of regulation khaki. What was even more remarkable was the fact that at 2.30 am they started to be tailed by something shining a spotlight on them as they drove along. Then the lights became dimmer, but simultaneously they were bathed in a brilliant light. A sudden wave of frostiness engulfed them, forcing them to wrap up and turn on the heater. (Remember Mrs Allan in Surrey?). Although Peter had taken his foot off the accelerator, they were still doing 150 km per hour. The inside of the vehicle was like a fridge, which was quite unseasonable for May. Even stranger was the fact that throughout this long journey there was no reduction in the speed which was being steadily maintained. The truth was that the car was out of control and failed to stop when required to do so by Peter. It was as if they were on automatic pilot with the steering wheel inoperative. The couple were in a state of panic, but Peter put on a brave front, saying 'It's only a UFO', as if it were the most natural thing in the world.

Shortly before they arrived at Fort Victoria the UFO left them. Matters had certainly taken a strange turn, and the very surroundings became distorted and unintelligible. They observed buses on a lay-by, deserted but with lights ablaze and their engines running. Such a thing is unheard-of in Africa. When they arrived at Fort Victoria's filling station the attendant pointed out a fault with their headlights, but was amazed to see the occupants of the car warmly wrapped on what was a hot night.

A sense of unreality pervaded the whole trip, but is typical of an ASC. A usually busy road was deserted and devoid of the normal considerable flow of traffic, while the terrain itself was transformed from one of sparse vegetation to a swampy and well-watered place with tropical plants and trees. Consistent with this psychological condition — in stark contrast to the hard facts of nature — all was eerily quiet, 'like travelling in a dream with all the sounds switched off;' this in spite of the fact that the radio was at first functioning normally. It seemed that someone else was still in control and the very road had been straightened out for them. There was no dawn or sunrise — just a dull grey sky, overcast and menacing in its unnaturalness. Husband and wife were as if completely under some very powerful hypnotic influence and when the radio stopped working Frances fell into a deep sleep.

When they arrived at their destination early in the morning, they were confused about the actual time of arrival, there being a difference of one hour: a time-warp was added to the general distortion of reality. All of a sudden the sun had arisen (but was it 7.30 or 8.30?), and there was no longer any trace of the UFO. According to his meter Peter had clocked up a mere 18 km, whereas they had actually covered a distance of 288 km. from their last stopping-place (Fort Victoria), and there was a correspondingly vast disparity in the amount of fuel used.

For some time Peter and Frances kept quiet to avoid ridicule. It was then revealed that Peter was no stranger to psychic experiences, OBEs in particular, which he considered relevant to his grand adventure and under hypnosis he talked about what happened when he was 'programmed' after his wife had fallen asleep. It seemed to him that a shape-shifting, fluid form was 'beamed' inside. That is to say, it looked like he wanted it to look, either pleasant or unpleasant, though such entities are physical beings at core. Apparently they are of a type basically human in appearance, but without reproductive organs. Their point of origin is to be sought in the inner and outer galaxies and they are well-disposed towards us, being extremely advanced in every way.

The alleged kidnap of *Travis Walton* ranks among the more controversial cases in ufology. It is set in Red

Indian Territory in 1975. A gang of woodmen had a contract with the Forest Service and were behind with their work. Sceptics have claimed that the whole story was invented as an excuse. As usual when there are claims and counterclaims, it is not easy to get at the truth.

The men were returning in a truck to their home-base in the picturesquely named city of Snowflake, some way off Phoenix, Arizona, when they observed a light among the pines that gave rise to various interpretations among them. A strange white-domed structure hung glowing motionless in the air. Travis jumped off the vehicle and walked towards the object to investigate. Whatever it was, it kept on beeping at a high pitch. It looked like a huge light-bulb and got louder and louder. Then it started to move and they observed a brilliant light. His colleagues, apparently less curious or courageous, fled in terror, leaving him behind to fend for himself as best he could. When finally they came to their senses they back-tracked to look for their friend, but he was gone.

When Travis's mother was informed of the incident she reacted suspiciously. A hoax, or even murder, was not ruled out but five days later the missing person rang relatives from a phone-box at Heber. Travis told his story of how he had found himself inside a saucer lying on his back in some pain with a light glaring from above. Giant creatures five foot tall with large bald heads and enormous brown eyes stared at him. As in similar accounts they lacked eyebrows, while their other facial features were poorly defined. Their dress was the standard ufonautical overall, here loose and orange-brown in colour. Travis knocked one over, being quite hysterical, and tried to ward off the aggressive entities with a tube that proved unbreakable. He managed to get up and walk in a futile attempt to escape. His next encounter was with someone of large size. He looked almost Caucasian in a close-fitting overall crowned by a large helmet that resembled a bubble and reached down to his shoulders.

In another room he came across two men and a woman with long dirty blond hair, who were very much alike. However, he was unable to converse with any of them. The customary medical examination was to follow when he was placed on a table and a kind of oxygen mask was put over his face. After this he became unconscious. He estimated the total duration of his absence at not more than two hours.

Philip Klass, an American aviation specialist and top expert at debunking UFO cases en masse, quotes several leading ufologists as denouncing the Walton abduction as if not as an actual hoax, then at least as unproven. Klass himself would pay $10,000 'to any 'UFO abductee' whose story is confirmed by an FBI investigation'. Others meanwhile have hailed this epic as the best-substantiated to date. Klass thinks that it is no coincidence that it followed hard on the Hill abduction which had received much media attention and was also poorly supported by external evidence. Travis Walton, on whose word we are solely dependent in our evaluation, is not a man of exemplary character, being apparently addicted to practical jokes in doubtful taste. Indeed, there are too many serious objections to this tale to make it wholly convincing as a true account of what he believed had actually happened. Even less are we inclined to embrace it as a factual, objective narrative of ET involvement in the trivial affairs of some rather unimportant persons in a remote part of the States.

We are on somewhat firmer grounds in the following account, though it may be thought to be no less way-out.

Antonio La Rubia, a bus-driver, lived not far from Rio. In the middle of September 1977 he got up very early in the morning on his way to work. Parked in a field there was what seemed appropriately enough to be a bus, but he soon realized that this was no ordinary vehicle since it covered the entire width of the terrain. About to make his escape, he was blinded when an intensive blue light lit up the scene to reveal three robots close by. He reckoned that they were no taller than four feet, but very long antennae stuck out from their heads. Indeed, they were not as usual since their heads were shaped like footballs with a band containing blue mirrors! A nightmare suggested by over-indulgence in SF could hardly have produced anything more bizarre. The creatures were covered by a scaly skin; their bodies were stocky, but their arms handless. These incompletely and grotesquely materialized forms showed only a single leg, each supported by a saucer-shaped platform like a stool. Antonio found himself paralysed by a light and caught inside an invisible container shaped like a bell jar. An object like a hypodermic syringe was pointed at him by one of the robots, who were floating around. The whole scenario resembled a chapter of a kids' comic rather than real life; an observation that generally applies to scenes from reports of UFO abductions and close encounters. At this point Antonio realized that he was inside a UFO with transparent walls in a large circular hall bathed in a bluish tint from above him. On either side he was surrounded by a dozen entities like children at school. To add to the absurdity of it all, he was unable to speak and when he tried to challenge his captors and jailers by screaming they fell down like so many toy-soldiers or ninepins.

The room was unfurnished except for something that might conceivably have been a piano but, as in a dream, it was pretty difficult to put a name to it. Next he was shown a series of extraordinary tableaux, in one of which he was presented lying naked and suspended.

Submitted to a peepshow of numerous other absurdities of a similar kind, a blood sample was taken from his finger with the ridiculous object of using the blood to draw diagrams on the wall. Finally he was 'teleported' to a place near a bus station. His watch had stopped at 2.55 am and he had all his belongings with him. It may be significant in view of his profession that his adventures started with the sight of a distorted 'bus', to end anticlimactically at a bus stop. However that may be, Antonio eventually deteriorated in health to the point where he had to give up his job with the bus company. His psychological condition gave rise to grave anxiety, while his physiological state was equally deplorable. In spite of all this, his doctor did not pronounce him deranged but, on the contrary, intelligent and most conscientious and, as so often in such cases, there was a happy ending when eventually his health took a turn for the better. It does not look as if his mental and physical ill health led to his imagining his abduction, but rather that a traumatic event brought on his temporary decline.

AntonioVillas Boas is the man who put sex on the UFO map, starting a new trend that had indeed been anticipated by the annals of witchcraft. His abduction took place in South America and was exceptionally well researched by the medical profession. It may have seemed unique at the time, but cases of alien rape have never been unknown.

The subject of this sensational tale (now deceased) is described by those who knew him as 'a typical small farmer of the vast Brazillian interior'. He had limited education but a high intelligence and became a solicitor. In October 1957 when he was aged 23 he saw something from his house at night. It was a kind of machine, round and luminous with purple lights and a blinding red 'headlight'. Its shape was that of an elongated egg with a revolving top and at its base it had a kind of tripod for landing: the sort of thing that has left apparent physical traces on the soil in some recorded instances. His tractor stopped dead (he was working in the fields). Antonio tried to escape by running away, but was grabbed by the arm. He managed to repel his attacker only to be tackled by three more, all small and in strange garb. Defying his protests, they carried him away puzzled by his resistance. Inside the craft he found himself in a small square room as if in bright daylight, after which he was ushered into a larger semi-oval one. His captors talked with bark-like noises that made them sound like animals. They undressed him, their ghastly conference apparently at an end. They rubbed liquid on him with a sponge and since it was very cold inside this primitive space-vehicle he began to shiver. Still more mysterious preparations were being made in yet another chamber, as part of which he was bled into a receptacle. He was then at last left to his own devices. They had provided a rather uncomfortable couch on which he sat down for half an hour or so, before becoming violently sick and suffocated by a nauseating smell of smoke that was pervading the whole room.

Villas Boas's description of the entities encountered by him runs true to form. They wore tight-fitting overalls and helmets. Tubes attached to these helmets ran into their garments, but did not have any obvious function other than a decorative one. They were evidently meant to suggest the use of diving-suits, so much in vogue in outer space, whether to deceive, or whether it is merely a case of ET fashion. Antonio goes into some detail concerning this uniform, including the small reflecting shield which they sported on their breast. Their gait was stiff and astronautical.

After a long uneventful interval Antonio was surprised when the door opened and he was face to face with a naked woman of unearthly beauty. She made no bones about her intentions.

This seduction scene followed the expected pattern. Caress followed caress etc. Her final gesture before leaving him was to point at her belly and towards the sky. Was the whole episode merely a dramatization of Villas Boas's unresolved emotional conflicts that gave birth to a dreamlike fantasy involving a more than usually attractive succubus? However that may be, the young man himself had ambivalent feelings towards the object of his enforced lust and regarded her as little more than a grunting animal, while being afraid of being kidnapped by alien forces beyond his comprehension. After she had left by the door his clothes were returned.

Antonio was diligent in digesting detail inside the UFO. He even tried to take a object as proof that he had really been there, but did not get away with it. Apparently the aliens do not wish us to have concrete proof of their dubiously objective existence. He calculated that he had spent 4 hours and 15 minutes inside. On his return to earth he found that his tractor — the one he had tried to escape on — had been sabotaged and still did not work. With a reticence neither surprising nor uncommon in such adventures, he originally only told his mother — his father would not have believed him anyway. He relived the trauma of his abduction in a series of nightmares and spells of nausea, and was not the first person of this kind to suffer from conjunctivitis. The strong sexual implications were to become more and more explicit a feature as time went on, and will be dealt with at some length later; they are, of course, standard in ancient accounts of witchcraft experiences with their associated allegations of incubus and succubus activities. The modern demons of ufology do not trail far behind with their unsavoury implications of rape.

Herbert Schirmer, a Nebraska patrolman, was alerted to a sighting in December 1967 by the erratic behaviour of the animals. Animals traditionally react to anomalies, often extremely violently, for reasons that are not quite clear. Very early one morning he came across what he thought was a truck, but changed his mind when the object flew away into the sky; yet another example of assimilation of the unknown to the familiar. Schirmer was a young man of 22 who had served in the navy. Flying Saucers were far from his mind at the time and he was hardly the type of man who sees a ghost in every bush in the dark, but now he had no doubt that he had seen one of those mysterious objects one hears and reads about. When he returned to his home he had a headache and was unable to go to sleep. He had also developed a red welt as if there had been some physical interaction — a common complaint that makes it hard to dismiss the phenomenon as 'all in the mind'. Indeed, things got so bad that he had to give up his job as a policeman and eventually undergo hypnosis. There are other cases where members of the police force have had this kind of experience, and they are usually considered to be of special interest. It transpired from the hypnotic regression that Schirmer had been paralysed and abducted. Inside the craft the light came from the ceiling, glowing with a red tinge in the control-room. The crew-members wore the usual silvery imitation divers suits with boots and gloves. The extra-terrestrials also lacked originality in appearance with their slanted eyes, flat noses and the merest suggestion of a mouth. The modes of communication used comprise *both* ordinary speech *and* some kind of telepathy. The humanoid aliens managed somehow to convey the idea of being 'from a nearby galaxy' with bases on Venus and similar likely places, others being on earth, with a bias in favour of the USA. It was explained to him how the energy driving the UFO is extracted from power lines and that it is made of pure magnesium. Perhaps all this wisdom should not have been accepted at face value as Schirmer was told that an element of deliberate disinformation was involved in this technical lecture on intergalactical space-travel via Flying Saucer. The case of the patrolman was investigated in depth and may be of some importance in unlocking the secret of the UFO enigma. It is not the first or the last instance of information being gratuitously given on the subject.

In a recent article in *UFO Brigantia* Peter Hough takes us 'Inside the Space Ships' and summarizes the technical information from time to time generously made available by our friends from Outer Space who are so pretentiously helpful at times and so actually scaring at others. But how many people know that in our own country there are no less than four factories that manufacture UFOs — in complete secrecy, but still known to Council tenant Stevens in Northampton? On the authority of the same person it can now be revealed also that they work on 'rotating currents', 'escapement mechanisms', 'electromagnetics', 'steam turbines' and 'mercury-operated make-and-break contacts'. Precise information on this subject was given long ago by contactee *Adamski* who acquired his education on a hamburger frying stand and who, according to someone who knew him personally, was 'a man of meagre scholastic attainment' though not lacking in imagination.

To return to encounters with aliens, they do not come more bizarre than what has been called the 'Flying Saucer Disease' of *Harrison Bailey*, an eccentric 24 year old American whose hobby was walking. In September 1951, Bailey was on holiday and on his way to Chicago and had to traverse a wood. He looked a bit like an extra-terrestrial himself, dressed all in green with goggles and heavy gloves. Approaching this forest he felt a pain on his back which he attributed to a whirlwind. It was not like anything he had ever encountered before, accustomed as he was to strange things happening to him on his peregrinations.

The next remarkable incident occurred inside the wood. There was what looked like a huge watertank, though more cylindrical in shape. An opening in it revealed two strange humanoids. The entities' faces were concealed by welders' masks and one of them demanded to know (in perfect English) where he came from. He answered truthfully that he came from Gary, Indiana on his way to St. Louis. This conversation was a bit of an anticlimax; he was not too keen on small-talk as he had a job to do and in a hurry to move on to the next stage of his journey. Although he suddenly felt very tired, he soldiered on, determined to put 'first things first.' Still he was rather puzzled to find that all of a sudden it was late in the afternoon.

He still had 25 miles to cover in order to arrive at Joliet before dark. Failing to do that, he arrived at a small place where he was put up by a station-master, and the following morning he felt much better for his rest. There was some hostility on the part of the locals; someone actually enquired whether he had come out of the flying saucer!

His life changed for the worse as the result of his encounter with the Unknown which he had so much taken in his stride. He became debilitated and sick, but the doctor's vague diagnosis was that he was suffering from a 'nervous stomach'. On the other hand, medical opinion agreed that he had aged at an alarming rate for a young man of 35 and in 1966 he obtained a disability pension, but gained little sympathy or understanding when he revealed what he thought was the real cause of his decline. Hypnosis apparently threw new light on his experience, revealing hitherto unexpected facets. Bailey, by now a minister of religion, had been attacked by frog-like creatures about 18 inches high with hand-like paws and three-toed feet. Their faces were featureless apart from the eyes and their mouths were mere slits. It was calculated that he had spent several hours in the forest, waking up inside a UFO on a soft bed. A bright light revealed the presence of machinery. More menacingly, two humanoids of bizarre aspect stood by him in what must have passed for the traditional post-abduction medical. Their attire consisted of a one-piece diving-suit. The traveller had little taste for this charade, which included 'telepathic' platitudes — which it took him fourteen years to recall. Whatever had been the object of the exercise, it had done him no good. He had undergone three time-lapses. It is worth noting in passing that recently a French case has come to light which makes one feature at least no longer unique since it involves frog-like humanoids with large glaring eyes.

Missing time also figures in the following which has been mentioned earlier. It involves a woman, her teenage daughter and a young man who were travelling together in the early hours of the morning in the autumn of 1975. The mother, *Sandra Larson*, had an appointment 200 miles from home at Bismarck, ND and left in good time to have breakfast before arriving at her destination at 8.30 am. However something very strange happened to put them off course. At 4.00 am they were surprised by the sound of a thunderous noise and the whole sky was lit up by an orange-glowing object. Unexpected though this was, something more inexplicable had taken place: Jackie, the daughter, was suddenly in the back seat of the car, whereas she had started the trip in the front between the two others. Moreover, when they looked at the clock it showed 5.23 — a whole hour or more later than they expected. The presence of orange objects in the sky was confirmed by people travelling along the same route.

Hypnotic regression once more revealed a lot of detail about the episode of Missing Time. It was an uphill struggle because of the subject's apprehension. A mummy-like figure had undressed her and X-rayed her stomach. Sandra also started to have strange dreams, while Jackie was affected by a sensation of weird presences within the house. Under hypnosis the daughter found herself paralysed in a field, separated from the rest of the party and with no idea how she had got back into the car: she 'just got there'. The hypnotist, Dr Sprinkle, was forced to 'exorcise' what seemed to be evil spirits causing the girl physical pain to the point where she burst into floods of tears. Sandra, in a further session by this experienced hypnotist who is very conversant with the subject, revealed that it was her belief that she had been operated on by the 'mummy'. There had been a momentary feeling as if her brain had been removed; it had been something to do with her sinus which had caused her a lot of pain previously. This is one of the exceptional instances of healing by the ufonauts, for she was now healed of her complaint.

In view of the resistance to the hypnotic probing it was only by gradual steps that the whole tale emerged in the course of several sessions. Sandra had witnessed the landing which had caused the car to stop. The UFO was the size of a 'big round house'; she was floated up into it as in an Out of Body Experience. There she saw her friend Larry strapped onto the table. Telepathy among ordinary mortals is erratic and unreliable as a form of communication, but once you enter the realm of ET enchantment it becomes the most natural thing in (or out of!) the world. She describes it as 'like the thought between two people, when you know what the other person is going to say'. When she eventually returns to the car, she and Jackie find that their vehicle is in a ditch and their memories have blanked out. Extraterrestrials go in for post-hypnotic suggestions, telling their victims to forget what they have experienced inside. They are, however, as inefficient in this as in other respects; and why should one not remember the dull and stupid lectures which they often go to such trouble to implant in our minds? When Sandra was floated into the craft she felt that it was a *physical* process, and not, as we have suggested, an OBE. Her investigators are satisfied that she had never been caught out. As far as it is possible to verify her statements, everything checks out. There is meanwhile the curious (but quite typical) fact that she can produce no witnesses to what is supposed to have happened on a normally busy interstate highway. It raises the problem of selective visibility (or sensitivity to) of manifestations which are very real to the percipient; Sandra, as we have just seen, considered her teleportation as within a purely physical parameter.

A fashionable coastal community in Southern California sets the scene for a more than usually incredible tale. The chief witness 'Hodges' is himself an investigator. *Dapple Gray* has the long-standing reputations for having been frequently visited by our friends 'from above'. It was about 1971 that this man and a friend met two dwarfish creatures. There is a certain measure of uncertainty about the chronology and about the exact shape of the aliens. On the other hand, there is no doubt in their minds that it was a harrowing experience. There was a loss of time, amounting to about a couple of hours. Under the skilful guidance of Dr McCall, who has made a name for himself in the hypnotic investigation of abductees, Hodges recalled two figures seen in the light of the car. One was larger, but both looked like 'Brains'. The exact date of the encounter was eventually established as 17th August 1971. 'Big Brain' conversed with the witness on matters of supposedly vital impact, but actually not out of character. Other entities, possibly subsidiary or subordinate to The Brain, are described as giants with grey skin and very thin yellow eyes and lipless 'pencil' mouths. Flat noses, as in the other cases, and hands with six spindly fingers, both hands and feet being slightly webbed. Their vests and trousers were of grey plastic or vinyl. They were towering presences at seven feet.

Hodges is generally considered to be an honest and intelligent person, sincerely searching for the meaning of this puzzling event. This is also true of his friend Rodriguez, who believed that his memory had been blocked out; a frequent assumption of abductees which does not stand up too well as we have already suggested. He was not easily hypnotizable and finally backed out from further investigation (in spite of his supposed interest), but his conscious recall, such as it was, agreed with what his friend said under hypnosis.

Bill and *Nora* were on their way to Los Angeles from Minnesota in the Summer of 1969. On reaching Salt Lake City at midnight the next day, the car went out of control, and it was not long before they spotted an object that made a humming sound. It was fish-shaped with a dome and had a red light. The car malfunctioned again to such an extent that they had the feeling that they were no longer in charge. They experienced a sensation of abject terror at being buzzed by the Unknown.

A snowman-like configuration with disjointed limbs came into view, but was visible to Bill only. The couple felt completely drained by now and were forced to take a rest by the roadside. It was at this stage that they noticed, not for the first time, a certain Ford camper. When the girl looked inside it she had the shock of her life: she was confronted with two creatures all covered in black leather gear, but minus their heads! A loathsome leering grin seemed to be superimposed on the merest outlines of humanity. The result of hypnosis even unnerved the hitherto sceptical inductor. It transpired that Nora had been beamed into the UFO, but did not like what she saw. On account of their insect eyes the ufonauts, engaged on her examination, resembled grasshoppers. It is the often told tale of the upsetting 'doctors' that mimic horror comics. The twenty or so diminutive semi-humans had green locust-like eyes and buzzed by way of conversing. There was therefore here no question of humanoids speaking perfect English or mastering the intricacies of telepathy, or even talking plain gibberish. Bill's (independent) hypnosis was complementary and even more detailed, but confirmatory of what came through via his friend. There was that same sensation of floating, experienced by both, which we have previously compared to an OBE, and at a late stage of the incident Bill was actually looking down on the car while still confined to the 'engine-room' with its ill-assorted collection of gauges and dials. The next moment he was back in the vehicle driven by Nora. Had he really ever left it?

Dr Kelly had done his very best to induce the couple to recall as much as was recoverable; always assuming with the investigators that there was recoverable material buried in their subconscious mind and possibly deliberately blocked. Bill was a behaviourist with little taste for the study of anomalies and anything paranormal. Both were deeply worried by the whole business. To be sure, their adventures must have been most unsettling when on the face of it time and space had been manipulated by a supposedly 'alien' force, the very existence of which they were unwilling to envisage even as a remote possibility. Jerome Clark, a seasoned investigator on whose account I have drawn for the main gist of the episode, calls it The Ultimate Alien Encounter, but you may be forgiven for thinking that each successive tale is so bizarre as to vie with the preceding for a description as 'ultimate'. What, for instance, is one to say of the following?

Lori Briggs is described by Rogo as 'an attractive UCLA graduate' who, when she was interviewed in 1979, was 'in her early twenties'. She was a young lady with more than one experience. The first had occurred when she was only sixteen and living in California. The story goes that she was dragged out of bed while asleep to find herself paralysed and sensing the 'presence' of some entities. ('Sensing' may seem incomprehensible to those who have never been subjected to the process: it feels very real at the time and simply does not involve the sense of sight.) Eventually they became more dense, enabling her to glimpse what was even then the merest shadow of a figure. As visualized by her, it had long thin white fingers and red glowing eyes which exercised a strong hypnotic effect on her. It is not inconsistent with a traditional apparition as recorded by the Society for Psychical Research, which has studied this genre for over a hundred years. And of course ghosts have been with us from the beginning of time. By 1975 Lori was living in a suburb of Los Angeles with a roommate, Jo Maine. It happened one night that Lori was communicating with an alien 'by telepathy', Jo meanwhile (although a sufferer from insomnia) sleeping heavily as if drugged. This appears to be a not uncommon side-effect and has indicated to some researchers that 'bystanders' are often incapacitated by the extraterrestrials so as to exclude them from the experience: here again we are hard pushed for a logical explanation. In any case, Lori was strongly urged to 'go with them', but was reluctant to do so; she found out afterwards that this incident coincided with a time-lapse. Her impression of large-headed white dwarves was once more by a process of sensing rather than actually seeing. There was coming from the kitchen a high-pitched sound that was heard by both women. A bright light outside was scaring Lori to death. She was not at that time thinking in terms of UFOs, but in the presence of the investigators she drew a sketch of a typical 'medical examination' such has time and again been reported by abductees. The girl specified that she had been hovering above the operation table, or what served as it, although she was unaware of the circumstances connecting this feature with the abduction syndrome. Indeed, it was not Lori but her investigators who made the crucial link, surmising that she had been taken from her home by creatures landed in a nearby field. Since that time reports of alleged kidnappings by extra-terrestrials have proliferated to an alarming extent.

Lori was advised to submit to hypnosis in accordance with standard American practice in these unresolved cases, and not surprisingly these suspicions were confirmed, at least to the investigators' satisfaction. The latter were all the more pleased with the results since it agreed with other accounts, notwithstanding the fact that the girl was a 'naive' subject who knew nothing of such matters from her previous studies.

She described how she was zoomed back instantaneously *à la* Star Trek, but as in cases of non-fictional teleportation also. (This usually applies to objects rather than to person, but the principle involved — if we are talking of actual events in real life — must be the same one.) There are also discrepancies with which we are familiar from similar accounts: the UFO arrives and lands unseen by anyone else in a very busy street, its almost blinding light is unobserved by the general public. It only gradually emerged that her flatmate had been simultaneously abducted, although her memories of the event were a trifle confused due to mental blockage by the aliens who, it is well known, go in for that sort of thing!

It was concluded that the case was unique in being not so much a double abduction as a *parallel* one, the two incidents being independent of each other: when Lori was kidnapped, Jo had been left behind. But are we talking in terms of physical events in relation to either incident? This, of course, is one of the enigmas we are setting out to investigate.

CHAPTER EIGHT

Cases involving the Police have always attracted special interest because of the presumed reliability of the experient. One such, from America we have already come across. *PC Alan Godfrey*'s encounter at Todmorden in West Yorkshire in 1980 is deservedly well-documented. In *The Pennine UFO Mystery*, Jenny Randles, Britain's only professional ufologist, chronicles how the Yorkshire village bobby, who is married with two children and with an excellent local reputation, and a sceptic with regard to our subject, was called out one morning in November 1980 on what initially turned out to be a wild-goose chase. A bright light appeared in front, which he presumed to be that of a bus. Why he should be tempted to investigate it is not clear to him. When he stopped his car at about 100 ft. from the light, escalation took its usual course and Godfrey found himself confronted with something altogether different. A dome-shaped object with a row of dark windows was hovering several feet above the road, the dome resembling a spinning top such as was popular with the very young at one time. Its five unlit windows contrasted with the bright shining surface of the craft. It was however the kind of brilliance that hurts the eye and makes close inspection impossible, and Godfrey could tell that it had a metallic surface reflecting his car-lights.

The constable acted in a truly professional way and, in accordance with his training, made an assessment of the situation, taking in as much detail as possible. He estimated its total length as 20 ft., and its height at 14. The lower part of the craft was spinning, rotating widdershins. Although it was a calm night, the bushes and trees were in motion, and Godfrey drew the obvious conclusion — though perhaps nothing can be taken at face value in this deceptive subject. He was unable to communicate with HQ, but this caused annoyance rather than surprise in view of the hilly terrain. (This factor could nonetheless be significant in view of the traditional electro-magnetic interference attributed to UFOs). Finally he made a drawing on his clipboard. The drawing was a valuable adjunct to further research of the case. As Randles remarks, a sketch is the next best thing to a photograph, and photographs of UFOs of undoubted authenticity are rare. Of course, if they are straightforward physical objects (as assumed by proponents of the ET hypothesis) this would be hard to explain. On the other hand, there is good reason to attribute physical components to them, so that there might well be genuine photographic (and cinematographic) records.

Godfrey's total experience, including his research, lasted for only a minute; sufficient time, it is reckoned, to do all he claims to have done. Real sightings are notorious for their short duration (like those of phantoms), and one distrusts those that are said to have extended over long periods of time. In spite of his coolness in the face of the Unknown, the policeman (as he freely admits) was afraid to leave the comparative safety of this car during the encounter. It was a natural rather than an altogether logical reaction. What is hard to understand is how he was transported inside his car over a distance of a hundred yards. It will be remembered that there are other cases of 'car-knapping', but

Godfrey was unaware of it. By then the UFO had disappeared. His sighting, however bizarre, was confirmed by colleagues in Halifax.

Hypnotic regression revealed an abduction scenario in which he was held down on a table and examined by hideous diminutive robots, while a six foot giant was studying him. The giant was dressed in a black and white sheet, bearded, and wearing a sort of skull-cap. The robots communicated by whistling to each other. Godfrey, again, was not supposed to remember anything, for he received the message 'You should not be seeing this. This is not for your eyes.'

Strange, incomprehensible creatures these aliens, and very alien indeed! Apparently it is a mistake to measure them by our own human standards as if we knew any others. They put on a show for our benefit which conveys little or no meaning to us, which we are meant to forget immediately afterwards. But the trick does not even work. Moreover, we are cast in the role of eavesdroppers, though we may have no intention to become a party to such strange and hurtful proceedings. One thing is certain, it was a most traumatic experience and a prolonged waking nightmare of the severest kind. So what are we to think of the authors of such terrifying scenarios? While earlier ufonauts were of a more benevolent type, like Adamski's suspect Venusians and the creatures encountered by the girl in Wales, hostile, or at best indifferent, dwarves suddenly replace them in about 1954.

A *young Venezuelan*, one of a party of three, was attacked by a small entity covered in hair, suffering physical injury by his hands. He and his pals made their getaway in a flat shiny saucer. As Donald Hanlon puts it, this looks like 'a deliberate and concentrated effort to confuse us, when you alternatively hear of "one-eyed giants", "hairy dwarves", "robots", "little men in luminous suits", "blond-haired and slant-eyed Christ-like beings" and so on.' At the time mentioned, there was a proliferation of small folk in France. It is also true that fashions change, from Zeppelin-shaped craft to round disks, as also among the occupants, and Hendry assumed on the basis of such divergence that 'the huge variety of appearances among the UFOs and the ufonauts alike support the idea that each is an individually imagined invention.' I do not, however, accept that the evidence supports so negative a view, inclined as I am generally to go along with his perceptive observations.

'Ufonauts — good, bad, or indifferent?' a basic problem to revert to. Villas Boas had good reasons to complain of a high-handed treatment by his captors, even though they laid on a sexual diversion. It was for their own good rather than for his benefit, for interbreeding and genetic interference is of the essence of the phenomenon according to one school of thought.

A controversial case is that of the men who went fishing in the Pascagoula River in Mississippi in 1973. They were allegedly struck by a buzzing sound coming from an egg-shaped hovering machine of large proportions. Three figures emerged and floated to them, humanoid, but otherwise featureless, as their noses and ears were conical, and instead of hands and feet they had claws. (We just note in passing that these features 'or lack of features' are not unique, and therefore do not seem 'individually imagined'). The two fishermen, *Higginson* and *Parker*, found themselves kidnapped into a craft to be scanned, leaving them paralysed. One of them was later subjected to regression. Lie-detectors were applied and tests successfully passed, but as is common in American cases, this only led to endless claims and counter-claims.

Randles was impressed by their sincerity, and this *cause célèbre* was never commercially exploited as by

111

some other abductees, but arch-debunker Philip Klass will have none of it. (Aviation expert Klass is the most outspoken critic of Budd Hopkins's theory of genetic engineering experiments allegedly conducted on abductees.)

Klass complains, among other things, that the late Professor Hynek (the doyen of ufology) accepted that the two men had 'a very terrifying experience' on the grounds that theirs had been a different kind. He also casts doubt on the nervous breakdown suffered by Parker and suggests that the whole story is a hoax, encouraged by the 'general acceptance of the previous (but quite different) abduction of the Hills, and its supposed hype of 'impressive scientific support'. Klass's evaluation of the data — so violently opposed to that of Miss Randles — is unfortunately typical of much that transpires in this field. People are boxed in in entrenched position from which there is no escape. In this respect they resemble religious and political fanatics, who may sometimes be 'on to something', but are by and large on the wrong track. This is not to deny that Klass and others never offer alternative views that may serve as valuable correctives to dogmaticism of a different direction as we shall see in our forthcoming discussion of the work of Budd Hopkins, Whitley Strieber and others.

The unpleasant aspects of the subject are once more to the fore in the adventures of an *American lorry driver*, in 1979. This man was attacked by a humanoid who could not be repelled by gun-shots, recalling the aliens of Kelly in Texas. He fainted, only to find himself at his destination (Fredricksburg). Reversing the tale of the South African journey to Beit Bridge, the 17-mile trip had consumed enough petrol to last for 117! When something was flashing over his truck that was identified in the usual way, the lights, the engine and the radio failed. There was also some damage to the vehicle. It was however suggested that the physical evidence was faked, and the case was regarded as inconclusive.

Two young people from *Maine* took a drive in the early hours of the morning. They complained of being buzzed by saucers with a blinding light. The result of this encounter was a number of physical symptoms of an unwholesome kind, but on the positive side it also rendered them 'psychic'. Under hypnosis one of them found that he had been the victim of medical test by entities dressed in white sheets of a peculiar appearance. Slanting eyes extruded from mushroom-shaped heads. Their facial features meanwhile were as often undeveloped.

A 19-year old *truck-driver* had a glimpse of a large rectangular object on his rounds in Kentucky in 1977. The radio malfunctioned and he lost control of the vehicle. A short drive had taken him 45 minutes and his eyes gave him trouble. Under hypnosis he 'recalled' a white circular room with no visible light-source. If this conforms to expectations, his 'doctors' *don't*: they were reduced to mere shapes; one white, the other two black. The unfortunate boy felt himself imprisoned in a test-tube and completely dehumanized: a case of biological engineering by superior intelligence of amorphic appearance?

Gilberto Ciccioli woke up in the early hours in 1974 in his Buenos Aires home to be blinded by a white light. A medical examination followed, so that we may assume that he had been abducted by a UFO. However, in this case his recall was spontaneous. Not everyone has to be hypnotized apparently to have the full benefit of alleged recollections while 'inside' a space-craft.

A man from *Tyler*, Texas, was surprised by two shadowy figures in 1977. The following day there was a shared sighting of a silver disc. As it turned out, this was not to be the last of his adventures, for two years on a sparkling 'beautiful beam of light' entered his bedroom, tingling as he touched it. This episode, subjective though it may seem, resulted in a time-lapse, since four hours later he was surprised to find himself sitting in his chair with all his clothes on. His general awareness as well as his psychic powers improved subsequently. Not all UFO experiences are wholly detrimental.

A young girl in her early teens went berry-picking near a French village in 1944. To her amazement there appeared an object, dull grey and looking like a small car parked on the grass. Two dwarves stood beside it dressed in brown. The child remained in a state of complete paralysis that lasted till the UFO had departed. (This again is rather like what happened to the school-girl in Wales.)

In 1950 in Dar-es-Salaam Mary, a five-year-old child was awoken by a vibrating sound. She said that a dwarf stared at her, but disappeared smartly when her father came into the room. Of course, this was all explained away as a nightmare, but unfortunately there were lasting effects that were both psychological and physiological, such as severe attacks of migraine. Ufology is not a very funny subject, cartoons of Little Green Men notwithstanding.

CHAPTER NINE

South American cases are a plentiful and Brazil in particular is a vast country rich in occult lore and phenomena. Guy Lyon Playfair, a leading psychical researcher, has recorded many cases of alarming but true happenings in the paranormal field, though not primarily interested in ufology. Early in 1975 a teenager, *Antonio Ferreira*, was attacked in his own home, reinforcing my previous argument that UFOs, whatever they may or may not be, are more than a pleasant diversion. Dark, diminutive creatures took him away and treated him with little consideration during a rough enforced ride to another 'planet'. Antonio was obliged to do a deal with them which, sad to relate, involved vivisection. Whether there is any truth in all this is another matter, but the case is no more suspect than some nearer home.

It used to be argued that UFOs were 'neutral', showing no hostility to us and not harming us except perhaps inadvertently. This is no longer believed to be so. Humanoids are deceivers and liars who scare children and other innocent folk going about their daily tasks and minding their own business, except for a minority caught up in UFO-cults. For every one cured there are literally hundreds who have suffered from inadvertent contact. At best they are laughed at; some lose their jobs. An American policeman took a photograph of a silver-suited alien which many researchers accept as authentic. It brought him no good luck: he lost his home, his wife and his job. Our own PC Godfrey has also reason to regret his encounter with a UFO. It is now alleged that ufonauts who kidnap and sexually assault humans implant devices into their bodies, and that there are cases of actual murder. However, before we investigate these more serious aspects, we must take a look at a typical side-effect of alien contact, the rather less disconcerting, but still annoying, interference with our concept of time: the time-warps.

Lost Time, the title of a recent study by American researcher Budd Hopkins, is by common agreement one of the hallmarks of the abduction syndrome. A familiar theme as in folklore, one of the earliest recent instances is connected with *Betty* and *Barney Hill* in New Hampshire. The couple were (eventually!) persuaded that their *Interrupted Journey* (the title of John Fuller's excellent account) had taken them an unreasonably long time — a time for which they could not rationally account.

At an even earlier date the *'Allans'* in their native Surrey were disorientated to the extent of missing a familiar bus-stop when they took what was to be a relaxing trip in the country. They were surprised at the lateness of the hour when they had their al fresco lunch near Wotton Church, while they hardly remembered their progress homewards. What had evidently been a most uncharacteristically traumatic event at the church for a case of haunting (for which, incidentally, there is not a shred of extraneous evidence) suggests that the lady conceivably had an abduction experience. Jenny Randles quotes several time lapses in *Abductions*. Some are from this country, but they are, as we have seen, a global phenomenon that knows no national or socio-religious boundaries, though they are unaccountably rare (or even unheard of) in some countries.

A *young engineer* in West Yorkshire on a desolate road across the moors was suddenly confronted by a glowing 'oval shape'. Paralysis set in with apparent loss of time.

A *Northamptonshire man*'s motorbike malfunctioned when a white light materialized beside him. Arriving at his destination, he complained that a period of 90 minutes had simply vanished into thin air — the way UFOs habitually function!

Americans can do even better in this field. The UFO experience is followed by 'momentary amnesia', and it is only at a later stage of recollection that the surprising fact becomes apparent to the experient. Usually it is only by the use of hypnosis that this is fully revealed. *Rev. Harrison Bailey* lost six hours of his life when he came across his frog-like entities. Hilary Evans has pointed out in this connection how time is 'overridden' and those favoured with 'bargain' interplanetary trips gratuitously bestowed on selected individuals do so within the briefest space of time, but sometimes pay a heavy price for this doubtful privilege.

The whole temporal concept is in a flux and from time immemorial it has been believed that people may enter upon a Rip van Winkle kind of syndrome in which it ceases to function in the accustomed way or becomes a downright irrelevancy. This is particularly true of shamans and shamanistic figures like the biblical Prophets and also of some mediums — in short, of anyone who enters either habitually or occasionally into altered states, one of which is of course the common dream-state, but includes trance. Thus *Elijah* escaped into a different time-continuum or dimension by being 'translated' by the divinity and could often not be located.

'Repeaters', in this context are not clocks that strike

the hour on demand but people like M. Masse who have repeated spontaneous UFO experiences. It is claimed that once contact has been established it is not easily relinquished. My friend from Wales still receives occasional visits at night from the aliens she came across one day in the country, although she is now a mother and has moved. A *Sussex girl* was about to get married when she was confronted by the sight of a flat greyish-green dome sitting on the lawn giving out a silvery glow. There emerged three creatures in khaki with bald domed heads, floating all over the place, but presently returning to base. Then, several years later, when she was living in Australia, she was nearly hit by a brilliant light. 1977 was the date when a *young mother* and her son were surprised by a giant in the ET uniform of a silver suit. Their neighbours made an unsuccessful assault on this strange sight, which was unusually prolonged, since it is said to have lasted for two hours, involving two policemen.

Late in September of the same year a *Dorset woman* observed a grey humming disc from her garden with two figures in silver suits inside. Her hands then turned red.

Time was when people saw cigar-shaped craft, but these seem to have gone out of fashion. A barrister saw one near Richmond, but only reported it to me because she did not know what to do with data of this kind. Kenneth Arnold started the disc-shaped saucer craze quite inadvertently by talking of craft that *skipped along like* saucers; soon everyone and his wife saw flying saucers along with other shapes.

Four *Cheshire poachers* talked of a 'silver balloon' from which emerged two entities, once more in silvery suits, but with the addition of miners' lamps. They seemed to take a more than passing interest in the cows that were grazing in the fields. Because of the unorthodox 'profession' of the gentlemen in question, the investigation was somewhat hampered. They were physically affected and probably spoke the truth about what they saw.

The next report takes us to *Sheffield*, and may seem superficially incongruous: a domed grey disc above, of all places, a fish and chip shop! This sighting is confirmed by a young widow and a man. Note that we are still in the realm of domed discs. The object contained a couple of ufonauts in ski-suits with long fair hair. The woman subsequently became 'psychic'. The early (1954) report by *Mrs Roestenberg* is almost identical to the one just given, but appears to be independent. It is possible that she observed the same event, which involved, according to her testimony, a shiny metallic disc with the same kind of entities. It was also seen by her children. The psychic parameter is once more in evidence.

Following on a display of unearthly pyrotechnics, a giant clothed in silvery garments interacted with a supermarket manager in Buckinghamshire. Supermarkets, Yorkshire fish and chip shops, they all come to life within the vast range of the UFO syndrome.

One of the strangest British cases is that of the so-called 'Mince Pie Martians'. Not only did these winged, weird creatures fly about *Mrs Hingley*'s living room, but she eventually started to float herself! If this were not such a well-investigated case one might hesitate even to record it. But sensations of being airborne are a common feature in UFO accounts as in near-death cases, and the frequency of floating dreams and so-called out-of-the-body experience (OBEs) need not be laboured. Telepathic communication with aliens may perhaps be linked with allegations of increased paranormal powers after contact, though people are to be warned against the assumption that telepathy is a reliable form of two-way communication.

Telepathic extraterrestrials date back to Adamski, whose books are full of occult pretensions of an unsubstantiated kind. For while it *may* be a fact that extrasensory perception is a form of communication, no message of more than a single word has ever been conveyed in this way in the laboratory. Even at this low level of achievement the evidence is precarious. ESP is a notoriously unreliable process that works at a *subconscious* level, while the idea that it is a viable alternative to conventional communication is unfounded. The nearest approximation to the concept of humanoid mastery of ESP impressed messages on humans — allowing for reservations regarding length and accuracy — is the marginal 'supra-lingual' telepathy reported by Professor Ian Stevenson.

It is also said that mothers have telepathic rapport with their offspring during the first two years of the child's life. It could be argued that this is merely loose usage in an attempt by percipients to describe an experience which it is impossible to talk about without actual articulation such as in sign-language. As such it might be said that there is a resemblance to the paranormal feats on record in poltergeist cases. Thus at Bristol at the *Lamb Inn near Lawford's Gate* about 200 years ago, mental questions were correctly answered by means of raps, even when put in Latin and Greek. Again, it has been assumed that mediums derive information which they are able to utilize in messages from the 'dead' to their clients by 'super-ESP'. This process is believed to function like a kind of radar picking up bits of information regardless of time and distance. We shall have to revert to the psychic aspects of the subject, as these seem to be relevant in many respects.

Albert Lancashire claims priority among British abductees as his adventures go back to the War in 1942 when he was on sentry duty in Northumbria. A beam of

Karen, another person with Merseyside connections, is a cook who claims the protection of a Guardian Angel, though perhaps not to the same extent as Nadia Mullen, whose 'angeloids' are myriads. Karen married and had a natural abortion accompanied by a shower of blood. This came as a great relief to her as she had been made pregnant in the course of an abduction by satanic forces — a theme that runs right through the ages and is now unjustifiably popular in America — starting with folkloristic belief in changelings substituted by the Little Folk.

A *multiple abduction* of three British women was thoroughly investigated by a competent researcher, a student of Sociology. The suggestion was offered that, being 'psychic,' they were prone to altered states (or fantasy-prone). One night in July 1981 they were being driven home from a night out. They had not been drinking. All observed lights, while one of the women thought she spotted a row of windows on a celestial object. The usual discrepancy of time was not resolved and hypnotic regression seemed called for. Unsurprisingly, this resulted in the memory of a medical by one of them. The unattractive aliens busy in their unappreciated task were only 4 feet tall and described as being hairless ugly dwarves with deep set eyes and spindly arms conforming to a pattern of 'little green men' in view of the colour of their cloaks. She was told not to be afraid — the aliens' sole customary concession to an otherwise far from humane conduct. The actual procedure was a cruel and painful one. The humanoids are sinister characters, unconcerned with human suffering. Another of their victims fared similarly inside the craft. However her ufonauts were faceless robots. There is thus a certain lack of agreement on this point, the more so as the third woman talked of giants with dark long hair, blue eyes and white skin; the so-called 'Aryan type'.

are noteworthy. On the way to Harrogate they noticed a melon-shaped object that had just 'landed'. There was talk of red lights being seen. Though these may permit a prosaic explanation, the failure of their car-radio at this precise point of time is more difficult to account for. A curious mixture of the normal and the abnormal, the easily explicable side by side with the unexplained, is a common syndrome of anomalous phenomena which has misled many an unwary investigator. The 'thing', which glowed a bright green, was estimated at 60 feet in length and half that height. Other drivers are believed to have seen it, but corroborative evidence under these circumstances is usually difficult to obtain. The silence that befell them was as unexpected by them as it is expected by us. Sandra got out of the car, but their memory of what now befell them is of the haziest. When they returned in the early hours of the morning the Police were waiting for them for questioning and later on Peter was interviewed by the MOD as well as by the Press. There were dreams about a man in yellow boots with a slit-mouth and piercing blue eyes. He was of small stature and Sandra describes his features as 'leathery'. These dreams were pleasantly reassuring. Peter claims to have subsequently been teleported in his car.

A Bristol man, *Keith Daniel*, describes how he had lived in an old house in Merseyside where he was plagued by a poltergeist; there seems to be a close connection between these physical phenomena; a point of contact dealt with later on. It could be just a coincidence, but one hears too many times of how people have suddenly turned 'psychic' after close encounters as the apparent result of their experience. However that may be, Keith now had dreams of being abducted by little men and had a number of weird encounters. At any rate, the investigator was impressed.

Before long he was aboard a bath-tub kind of flying machine to be subjected to the usual procedure.

The case of the *Janos People* is claimed as an early British abduction at Faringdon in Berkshire. Unfortunately it was ineptly investigated and the material recovered under hypnosis was contaminated by the hypnotist leading the witness. It became the subject of a book by someone who believed in the literal truth of every item revealed by that dangerous technique and whose qualifications leave much to be desired. Unsurprisingly, surgery rears its suspect head in the narrative.

Linda Taylor was driving on a usually busy road near Manchester when all of a sudden there was a deadly calm — a familiar prelude. She found herself paced by an enormous light causing interference with the normal running of the car. This light changed into a metal disc and was seen by the petrol station attendant. Psychic experiences and a time-lapse complete the story.

The following case is of more than usual interest because it was extensively investigated at great expense. This unfortunately is an exception as most research is done by part-time amateurs on behalf of small private outfits with little financial back-up. It is also extremely time-consuming if properly followed up. The 'UFO Collision' of Minnesota involved the police. Deputy *Val Johnson* crashed his patrol car under mysterious circumstances under attack from 'a highly charged electrical thing'. Temporary damage to his eyes suggested a mild dose of radiation and it was concluded that a strong electrical charge had ionized the air. The question arises of how, why and by what? This remains an unsolved mystery in spite of the care taken to solve the riddle. A time-lapse is included as well as other related incidents, but does not help to clear it up.

Reports concerning a young couple, *Peter* and *Sandra*,

yellow light struck him and he felt that he was floating. Later on he realised that he had been inside a UFO and psychic occurrences, some at least objective, took place. The fact that basically there is nothing new is shown by the realisation that even earlier instances have been dug up by investigators. Jacques Vallee came across the account of a teenager who, in 1928, saw a UFO with rivets. Through a window of this rather primitively constructed but apparently efficient, craft he espied an Italian-looking man in uniform. But then, Dr Vallee points out, practically all cultures have traditions of abducting airships.

Mrs Vernon wasn't far from Wellington when her car seriously malfunctioned. She became unconscious after seeing a metallic giant with a flashing light. The disc had the familiar dome. Then came the equally familiar medical by men in skull-caps, face-masks and aprons — a passable imitation of rather callous surgeons. But also old hat in stories of abductions. She could not shake off the impression that she was treated without any real compassion, no better than laboratory animals as subjects for vivisection. Worse still, she felt that she was being raped — the constant theme of the much later period.

A long and involved tale hangs on the misfortunes of *Shelley*, a Bolton teenager who claims to have been in close contact with a UFO. The girl suffered in various physical ways, with burns, soreness of the eyes and spells of dizziness. Her teeth were also allegedly affected. Psychic parameters included floating. An instance of actual levitation is independently attested. Shelley also 'lost' 45 minutes. A medical examination was conducted 'inside' by a tall, blond female.

A Yorkshire *ambulance driver* had an unwelcome visit at home by a couple of disagreeably arrogant beings of large size, grey-faced with big feline eyes.

Hairy dwarves feature in the literature as well. For some unexplained reason, there are two in close proximity in South America in December 1954 and few afterwards. As presented, they are furtive and decidedly unpleasant fellows. *Two teenagers* out on a hunting expedition in Venezuela were surprised by four hirsute entities of about 3 feet that emerged from a disc to capture them. The gun used by one of the boys broke. The police concluded that they had been mauled by savage beasts. How can one account for the coincidence that only six days later another man had to be rescued from a similar monstrosity in a park by a friend? And in the same year of these sparse but uncanny observations of dwarf-like creatures unfamiliar to natural science, there was a regular glut of them in far-distant France.

From the same part of America, but in 1965 come reports of hairy blue-eyed giants with white complexions with a penchant for interbreeding like members of the SS.

Three excellent witnesses, including a *gynaecologist*, were discussing business at a stable near Caracas. Surprise and terror was their initial reaction to a humming sphere that arrived in a blinding flash. Two outsize 'Aryans', 7 foot tall with long fair hair and large round eyes appeared dressed in metallic suits and tried to calm them down. They were accompanied by 3 foot tall creatures of uncertain function. The avowed mission of the giants was to stop a 'plutonium explosion'. Does this mean that we have to face up to at least two distinct extra-terrestrial races differing in height? But even this way-out hypothesis would be insufficient to account for the data. True, such naive assumptions were acceptable at one time. One has only to glance at the early paperbacks to find it seriously suggested that superior intelligences, from goodness knows where, alarmed by our technical advances in means of mass destruction, were hastening to our planet with good intentions such as often proclaimed by the ufonauts.

The big fellows are also appear in a sighting by a retired *Argentinian air pilot* who may have entered into an altered state while sitting in front of the 'box'. Right in front of the astonished man was the silent seated figure of a giant in a green metallic overall with slanting 'Oriental' eyes. To the touch it felt rather like foam-rubber! Its apparitional nature was more evident than its association with alien craft in view of the fact that the figure eventually just vanished and therefore failed to interact, except visually, with the drowsy pilot. The same type of alien, tall in stature and with 'Oriental' eyes, was seen by a compatriot of the pilot. *Dionisio Llanca*, a lorry driver, met up with a hovering disc with three inmates, two male, one female. A triad of configurations, perpetuated in a drawing on the cover of FSR, is typical of landed saucers, but not ghosts, who prefer to manifest singly. While their voices were weak and squeaky, their 'medical' made up for it by being all but gentle. Dionisio was subjected to traumatization with total amnesia according to his doctor's diagnosis. His allegation that he was paralysed by a yellow beam of light and his subsequent ordeal at the hands of the aliens could not be shaken by the investigators. Under hypnosis he told a tale of being transported to a bright room where he was lectured on the dangers to our planet, a subject that has been exhausted by the environmentally orientated. It is, however, relevant to insist on the obvious fact that these exhortations nearly always reflect current thought and preoccupation such as nuclear threats to the Earth.

In the same neck of the woods *Carlos Diaz* was returning from work at four o'clock in the morning when he imagined that he heard a loud hum, followed by a blinding and paralysing flash like St. Paul's on the road to Damascus. Floated up he found himself inside a craft. A figure clad in an overall and wearing a balaclava helmet approached him and removed some of his hair using a suction device. Like the Argentinian pilot he noted that the 'doctor' felt like rubber! Carlos came to at 8 am to find himself by the road from where he was taken to a hospital, having travelled no less than 300 miles from Bahia Blance to a location near Buenos Aires. To his credit and adding credibility to his story, he refused to cash in on this remarkable incident but generously allowed himself to be fully questioned.

Whatever happened to *Corporal Valdes*? The case is authenticated at the highest level but remains impenetrable and enigmatic. He is supposed to have been abducted on a Chilean desert plateau. It all started off when a soldier observed a couple of descending violet lights illuminating the terrain. It turned out to be a mysterious object with one large central light and two smaller side ones when it vanished out of sight. Shortly afterwards the corporal returned home in a state of trance, muttering an obscure message that bore little resemblance to what had happened and shed little light on it. He then passed out.

His watch had now gone berserk! It had stopped and showed a date several days in advance. Investigation by journalists was cut short by his General. He suffers — or claims to suffer — from complete amnesia. Perhaps he has not revealed all; if so, it is in character for people who have been privileged with encounters with entities, whether secular or religious.

The sexual connection with this subject is one that cannot be overstated, since it turns up again and again throughout the ages and in the most diverse cultural contexts. It therefore comes as no surprise that a *teenager* remembered under hypnosis how sex was forced onto him by a tall silver-haired woman with large eyes. The boy, *Jose Alvaro*, is Brazilian. In 1979 he was 'struck by a blue beam' that affected him strangely. In partial corroboration it is reported that a light had been independently seen at the same spot and that Jose himself had been observed by a passer-by on the ground.

An outstanding case from Brazil has two witnesses to it. It happened two years later, when a *concert pianist* and a female student were travelling along a coastal road at night. A domed object with three lights came into view over the sea. This was a strange coincidence as the two had just been discussing flying saucers. Returning from Rio, which was where they had been heading, more lights caused a commotion in the water and even interfered with the car's mechanism. It is not quite clear from their description what it was they saw next, except that they considered themselves to be under attack. It was now 11.30 pm and the whole landscape was lit up; for some reason or other they were in a state of absolute panic followed by a period of amnesia. Their Fiat 147 was partially magnetized and the artist's watch was no longer reliable. The woman's eyes were red and she suffered some internal trauma.

The surgeons that almost invariably take the stage under hypnosis were of diminutive size with grotesque features, but perhaps one should not pitch expectation too high with denizens owing allegiance to somewhere 'near Neptune'? A poor joke? A naive attempt at deception? Psychical researchers are well acquainted with both in their specialized studies of anomalies of which ufology is just another. The musician realized that his captors were talking nonsense.

Abductions take place by preference in the open, but it must not be thought that you are safe from the attentions of aliens in your own home. They are as capable of penetrating its walls as witches and sorcerers in bygone ages. *Joao da Silva* in Brazil can not have felt threatened when he took a drink from the kitchen tap one night. Notwithstanding his sense of security in his 'castle', he was reluctantly floated away to be tempted by a naked woman. Interbreeding is considered very desirable (or perhaps essential for survival) by some non-human race in the Universe, but what actually happened inside the craft is uncertain since Joao lost consciousness (or possibly was too embarrassed to remember). Next morning he was found lying naked on the floor with red marks on his skin. His watch had stopped and there were poltergeist phenomena in the house.

Antonio Tasca was the victim of pale-skins with slanting eyes. As so painfully often, they could not refuse the temptation of giving a 'message' for the world. A doctor had no explanation for the burns on Antonio's back.

The adventures of *'Jennie'* from Nebraska have all the hallmarks of a dream, a fact of which she was fully aware. Like Joao, she was in her home. Wearing only a nightgown, she floated to an alleged business session inside a vehicle with a tendency to fade and become transparent, a feature also noted by Bob Taylor in Scotland. Her aliens were midgets, the leading character being distinguished by a kind of bathing-cap — possibly to disguise his lack of hair — on top of an egg-shaped head with a pale waxen face. Another common feature: nose and mouth were barely defined. This also applies to the slit-like eyes, which are nowadays (following the trend set by Strieber) rather large. The girl was clamped on a silver table by her examiners. In this early case (1955) there is also a physical trace. Next day an elm tree outside her window was found to be burnt.

A New York State *nurse* suffered from symptoms that puzzled the doctors and a gynaecologist. Under hypnosis she relived a sexual assault by fair-skinned hairless dwarves, showing once more that allegations of rape by extra-terrestrial and similar entities are part and parcel of the abduction syndrome. Meanwhile a case can be made for an extension of Rupert Sheldrake's theory of 'morphic resonance' which eliminates boundaries.

A British case from Telford is almost duplicated by one from Kentucky. There were three female abductees travelling together by car. But only one, *Mona*, had much recall under hypnosis when she remembered white-clad persons seemingly engaged on a gynaecological test.

There is a certain predictability, not to say monotony and lack of inventiveness, in such accounts, which has persuaded some that there is a prototype which is slavishly followed by subsequent hoaxers; but this is a wrong reading of the data which have a timeless and culture-unrelated quality in their essentials. Small wonder then that in a Canadian account of similar experiences *Jack*, a member of a rock group, tells of a number of interferences starting at the tender age of two. In 1971 Jack and a friend were finally accorded the doubtful privilege of meeting small aliens with the usual interest in the human body. Is there some kind of affinity between the phenomenon and the musical profession? Jenny Randles thinks so: a theme recently taken up by Werdna Strebor in an article entitled *Rock Music & UFOs in UFO BRIGANTIA (No 44)*, who says that 'a great many rock musicians . . . have had UFO experiences or feel strongly about the subject and have set these thoughts down in their lyrics or interviews'; including John Lennon.

An early account dates back to 1951 and is located in Cape Town, South Africa. A *British engineer* went for a late-night spin in his car. He met a mysterious stranger who requested water. The person was small, dressed in a brown overall; his domed head was hairless. The engineer got an invitation to inspect the space-craft, but seemed to have lacked somewhat in curiosity or enthusiasm. The water was apparently wanted for someone who had been burnt — which you are free to believe if you must! There is some resemblance in this tale to the familiar ET scenario.

Africans from tribal Zimbabwe interpret their aliens in accordance with their own belief in ancestral activities. Assimilation meanwhile still runs on rational lines, and a glowing disc was attributed to a forest fire by the *foreman* until, that is, he was confronted by three tall entities in the silvery garb familiar to us from other non-tribal reports and paralysis started to set in. The African had not even heard of spacemen from earth, let alone flying saucers. But his observation in the course of everyday duty did not fit in with his usual experience any more than if he had been a European or American, and the anomaly, once appreciated as such, gave rise to the familiar psychological process of escalation of hypothesis.

Ufologists are thin on the ground in the vast tracts of the African continent. One report speaks of a 56 year-old *South African* who alleges a long-standing contact with alien visitors. He claims to have been abducted by creatures with large hairless heads who placed him on their operating table. He further accepts as a fact that he has newly found psychic faculties due to an implant. This, at any rate, is something new. It is frequently alleged that the UFO experience has this side effect, but the precise mechanism by which this comes about is left obscure. The man was informed that his aliens were not hostile, but are they to be believed? A rare *Japanese* case conforms to the usual pattern. There is the orange beam and the small monster with a barely suggested nose whose victim suffers temporary paralysis. It is also in line in involving interference with the car engine and the radio and the fact that the watch stopped at the critical time. There is also a claimed implant, the purpose of which is to contact him in the future, recruiting him as an additional member of the army of 'repeaters'.

Another Asian, this time *Chinese*, is a truck-driver who saw a blue glowing dome on the road with two midgets in silvery dress. They were armed with lamps and torches but were shy on being pursued, disappearing abruptly. We are meant to think that this minimal contact was unintended, just as the Little People of old have been surprised in their cavortings by unwelcome human observers who 'just happened to be there', but we prefer to keep an open mind on this subject.

However far afield one wanders, the phenomenology does not substantially diverge from the usual pattern. Can it really be due to simple imitation? Do the inhabitants of distant lands all over the world slavishly copy each other's pseudo-experiences with the object to deceive, or are we face to face with what Rupert Sheldrake has taught us to accept as Morphic Resonance, a kind of ESP that travels without physical limitations to the collective unconscious?

In *Réunion*, in the Indian Ocean, a young shop-assistant watched as a domed object landed in a field while dwarves immobilized him with a white beam. Their ostensible justification for such a long trip was to collect soil samples. He suffered from aphasia and, as he was unable to speak, the usual communication did not take place; also his vision was temporarily impaired as with the woman whose Midlands house was invaded by the winged creatures. Medical opinion confirmed that the man had had a severe shock.

Cultural variations in abduction scenarios do meanwhile occur. In Asian cases the UFO presence is unattested; the entities 'just step out of their reality [or dimension] into ours'. (Jamaludin). This is also true of the instances so far examined where the presence of the craft is extrapolated on more or less compelling grounds. And, of course, it agrees with European folklore which ante-dates the Flying Saucer craze. A man in *Western Australia* was in his car at night when both the motor and the radio began to cause trouble, ultimately to grind to a halt. An oval shape hovering above him struck out with a blue beam. (Note in passing how it is always a 'beam' with variations in colour of the light!) He seemed to have entered into another dimension in which there was a temporary suspension of sound which Jenny Randles has christened the Oz-effect, basically an altered state. After some time the light was no longer there and he continued his journey. It had affected his Omega watch and he suffered from attacks of migraine to which he had not previously been prone, though his psychiatrist could find nothing organically wrong with him.

A possible abduction of an Aborigine is uniquely reported from *New South Wales*, where there had been many reports of UFOs. This man saw a small entity through his kitchen window which had previously been shattered by a blast and he was sucked out and found lying on the ground.

Another example of the white light: in 1974 a *musician* accompanied by a boy was struck by it out hunting; there was a humming sound. An Oz-factor is suggested by the fact that all other sounds were cut out. The investigator surmised that the original stimulus was a star — many extraordinary adventures are triggered off by trivial stimuli such as seeing Venus. However, years later the youngster had dreams suggesting the usual 'medical' of the abduction syndrome.

Other European records include the following.

A twenty year-old maid in *Romans* (France) was

returning from the cinema when she had trouble with her car. She noted that the sky was glowing yellow. She lost several hours on her journey and under hypnosis told a tale of having been examined by big-eyed, ugly dwarves.

An *Italian peasant* encountered an 'upturned egg' accompanied by two big-eyed midgets who robbed and paralysed her. This is an unusually interesting account as both the UFO and the aliens were independently attested by outsiders.

A *young Italian* in the Dolomites saw tall, dome-shape headed ufonauts with Oriental eyes who communicated by ESP, being very concerned about the possibility of the earth's crust cracking!

This is obviously a worldwide phenomenon, whatever may be its explanation, with many European instances. Thus a *Swede* had a very traumatic experience in 1974 when a blinding flash of light disabled him temporarily. There were burn-marks on his cheek. At a psychological level this was also confirmed. Regression induced extreme terror at the sight of tall hooded figures who were trying to do something to him with an instrument. Subsequently he became gifted with ESP and PK.

Jan, a Polish farmer, had never even heard of flying saucers. Yet when his horse and card were brought to a halt by aliens with Oriental eyes he found himself up in the sky, travelling via a tube. Having been medically examined he was allowed to depart. He had complete normal recall, just like Burtoo of Aldershot.

A *Russian officer*, described as 'high-ranking', was met by two entities in dark cellophane suits who talked with him at some length 'by ESP'. Psychologists believed him, and he was not charged.

A *Finnish woman* in her car was caught up in a mist and transported to a place where she was examined by obnoxious small creatures. This was in 1980, which is a little surprising in view of the fact that gynaecological problems were discussed, an aspect of ufology that has only recently come into its own.

A *young farmer* and his girlfriend in *Spain* were walking along a dark lane when they came upon a hovering craft whose powerful beam knocked them out and blinded them. Two tall thin figures terrified the farmer, who was found to have red marks on his cheek.

Another *Spaniard*, this time a vet, was also subjected to a strong light. His entities were tall but Nordic in appearance and were interested in his dog. His eyes were affected by the encounter and he learned of the existence of two disparate types of ufonauts, the other kind being small and ugly and preoccupied with genetic engineering without showing undue scruples, perhaps reflecting our own (human) unease with some modern medical developments, regarded by some as two-edged swords. There is indeed good reason to think that ufology projects our own preoccupations and basic universal worries and doubts.

How do animals react to anomalies? It is often claimed that people are alerted to their presence by the violent behaviour of domestic animals and beasts, such as barking, or restlessness on the part of their cows. According to Prof. Hynek, the doyen of ufology, 'animals sometimes become aware of the presence of the UFO even before human witnesses.'

Alan Hendry, who worked for Hynek's organization, tended to be sceptical. He mentions this aspect in a chapter of his excellent study under the heading of 'Tools'. Of course, animals are more sensitive to a variety of physical stimuli than humans and are thus an important 'tool' in the observation *in advance* of earthquakes for example. It is well known also that birds use the earth's magnetic field for navigation, while bats find their way about in the dark by sonar. But while all this is common knowledge, what influences animals when it comes to the elusive presence of the UFO? As Hendry points out they do not fantasize, and are therefore more 'naive' even than the native of the most remote region of the world where the concept of space-travel is unknown. Animals 'sense' what humans may not be aware of. In short, can they perceive 'with hearing that ranges into the ultrasonic sounds made by a UFO? Can they smell odours, detect microwave energy, low-strength magnetic fields, or small static charges?'

Hendry thinks that the relationship between the presence of a 'Flying Saucer' and animal reaction is a myth of the American people and that they may be so closely 'attuned' to us that they react to our own moods and preconceptions. This theory is not borne out by the study of apparitional and other psychic phenomena. Nor is it suggested by Dr H Heaton's collection of over 200 sightings. The Goffstown (N.H.) case of 1973 is of special interest as a contact with aliens is alleged. Two humanoids in silver suits were gathering soil samples in a backyard. The owner set his guard dog on them, who attacked them in a very half-hearted way before beating a retreat into the house where he lay down whining. Project Blue Book seems to have been impressed by what happened in New York State in 1965 when a silver disc descended near a farm, turning the clouds green. Apart from its strange appearance (it had red glowing streamers and a red-yellow tail) it beeped, smelled of burning gasoline and interfered with the AM radio. A dog barked, a cow gave less milk (as in witchcraft cases), and a terrified tethered bull made frantic efforts to break loose. No wonder no pat explanation was forthcoming!

Animals are attuned to the paranormal. All the evidence suggests that the awareness of the pet often *precedes* that of his master and cannot therefore be attributed to his unease *vis-a-vis* the Unknown. There are no cases explicable by the standard interpretation of 'infection' from timid Man to Beast as believed by Hendry. When towards the end of the last century the founders of the SPR set themselves the task of discovering whether animals were affected by paranormal phenomena, the unequivocal result of their investigation was that they were indeed in an overwhelming number of cases. In fact, this proved to be so in 'every case' recalled by them. Frederic Myers declared point blank that he was not aware of any instance where pets failed to show terror at 'phantasmal sights and sounds'. Humans react in a number of ways, ranging from faint amusement, curiosity and unease, to downright fright. More recently, the International Journal of Paraphysics published a thousand cases of hauntings and poltergeists over a period of ten years. They involved dogs, cats and horses.

In statistical assessments canines are in the majority. Among 100 dogs, no less than 95% are reported to have shown hostility in their approach to the phenomena. There are also examples of extreme cowardice, with dogs reduced to a 'state of terror'. One 'showed every symptom of fear and anger.' Dogs described as 'savage' by their owners (including guard dogs) are 'paralysed with fear' in haunted houses, while presumably paranormal noises reduce them to a state of 'abject terror', so that they 'cower' or tremble violently in a most uncharacteristic manner. A particular frantic canine is even said to have jumped through a window to be killed by a passing car. Another shattered a pane of glass in its headlong flight. Red Indian tradition has it that dogs and horses are afraid of ghosts. There are fewer data for cats, but they confirm the finding with dogs and horses.

The dog's unusual response in particular thus belies his traditional image of courage and faithfulness in this respect. Growling and barking dismally, he cringes, runs away and hides, or even (in rare cases) does serious injury to himself in his panic. On the whole, the animal's behaviour is independent of, and often in marked contrast to, that of his human companions.

CHAPTER TEN

UFOs have always been acceptable to (if not actually welcome) by the self-appointed experts, but sightings of ufonauts were for a long time 'out'. This may seem all the more strange since flying saucers were regarded as piloted ET craft; so why no pilots? Or perhaps the idea of spaceships from other planets was a sufficiently daring concept without being contaminated by the idea of little green men invading Planet Earth. It is of course only a logical extension, it being difficult, to think of the one without the other. But what are they like?

We have by now gathered sufficient evidence to show that not only are they inconsistently portrayed, as well as being almost consistently ridiculous. They indulge in ludicrous activities, often mimicking us by taking soil-samples like our own astronauts on the moon, while affecting a garb with a pretence of it being mandatory for visitors from planets with other atmospheric conditions.

Yet by and large, ETs — of whatever size — are not unlike us in general appearance and seem to manage quite well without their prominently displayed breathing apparatus. One such creature had nothing better to do than to survey the backyard of a workman's house in industrial Belgium! The strange fairies of Mrs Hingley made a thorough nuisance of themselves and talked childish nonsense: a favourite occupation of some of their kind. But there is surely something rather unpleasant about these deceitful and mocking creatures who invade our living-space and even the privacy of our homes (including our bedrooms), even if they assure us that they mean no harm. And don't they! At the lowest level, they interfere with our free flow of movement, cause appliances to malfunction and are frequently responsible for paralysis and physical discomfort.

An extreme example is the suffering endured by two American ladies. One, Betty Cash, was severely burned with radiation symptoms that have persisted to the present day. It is therefore wrong to maintain that no crime is involved. But is there something even more subtly sinister with wider implications? American artist and author Budd Hopkins argues the case for actual assault with implants by aliens, while others object to this theory as a 'dangerous game' that imperils the mental health of large numbers of so-called abductees in America and elsewhere. Missing Time, according to Hopkins, provides the clue, as do also certain lesions on the bodies of the victims. Strangely, something similar is also found on victims of murder supposedly reincarnated according to the data provided by Prof. Ian Stevenson. Or are they akin to a well-known phenomenon of psychology: the enigmatic stigmata?

There was much talk of the Devil's Mark (*stigmata diaboli*) in the late Middle Ages — alternatively known as the Devil's Seal, and Robbins, an authority on Witchcraft, complains of a frequent confusion with the Witch's Mark, which a contemporary writer had denounced as 'mostly deceits of the torturers'. Although used interchangeably, they are basically different: the former is 'a scar, birth-mark or tattooing', whereas the latter is nothing more than a protuberance that was believed to be sucked by the 'familiar' or imp (a pet kept by witches, but suspected of being an instrument of evil.) Both are natural parts of the human body perversely misrepresented by demonologists. There seems no point in lingering over the monkish and salacious details relating indelicately to the process of searching them out, or their purported detection by 'pricking', whether fraudulently or otherwise. These in their turn are to be distinguished from the 'indelible mark' made by demons at the Witches' Sabbath (the *striacium*). Giovanni Sion, on being asked by an Inquisitor whether he had been branded by the Devil, explained that it had been done with a branding iron, but had been quite painless. A round scar on the right side was pointed out by way of irrefutable proof that he had indeed attended the Sabbath, it being 'real and in no way an illusion.' So also a lesion of obscure origin is in our own enlightened days seen as cast-iron proof of the physical interference by ETs or, alternatively, as evidence of the reality of Reincarnation.

Our modern concept of stigmata is different; summarily relegated to the realm of psychology and the subconscious level of the mind. They are again distinct from the 'scars of bodily penance' of the religious fanatic, and the simulated variety discussed by Ian Wilson.

Prierias, who wrote extensively on the subject of Witchcraft in the first quarter of the sixteenth century, makes no mention of stigmata, but the earliest case that may be relevant to this discussion is much more ancient.

A man who bore on his hands and feet the wounds of the Saviour was summoned before the Council of Oxford in 1222 when Stephen Langton was Archbishop of Canterbury. A female associate was accused of having magical powers.

Stigmatization occurs in conjunction with hysterical subjects, but need not necessarily be pathological. Its symptoms — relatively common among mystics — were to play a disastrous role in the propagation of the witchcraft mania which, some would argue, extends to the present enthusiasm for UFO abductions. Hilary Evans has drawn an illuminating parallel between Witchcraft (which he regards as totally delusory, and the UFO syndrome which is, to say the very least, inconsistent in its manifestations). Evans wonders whether the phenomenon, if not striking indiscriminately, searches out certain individuals, or whether, on the contrary, the individual searches *it* out. However that may be — and it is clearly an important question — Michaelis, like Sion, could argue in 1582 that the physical nature of the Devil's Mark showed that this was no mere delusion or dream, just as the allegedly hard data are said to prove the physical reality of the syndrome, supported as they appear to be by the testimony from different and widely dispersed countries and cultures, and extending by now over a vast stretch of time.

Elizabeth of Belgium, an ecstatic and stigmatic nun, was 'in an almost continual state of trance' in which she enacted the Passion of our Lord in her own body. At a time when demonic powers were universally accepted, few doubted that the origin or her state was to be looked for in that direction, though the Church was obsessed with the suspicion of fraud. And it is also true that stigmatization by itself is no guarantee of sanctity. The sacred name of Jesus was engraved upon the breast of the Blessed Eustochium, but strangely attributed to the devious devices of Satan. (Similar things are also done by Indian fakirs.) The stigmatic impression of two sixteenth century 'imposters' are deserving of note since they made a clean breast to the Holy Inquisition — not that such confessions have to be accepted at face value. People readily confessed to imaginary crimes like flying on broom-sticks and to others of which they are known to have been innocent. Even Eustochium believed the charge of Witchcraft levelled at her in spite of strong contrary indications of holiness.

'The most extraordinary manifestations' of Palma D'Oria, including pretended stigmata, were denounced by the Holy Father himself as the work of the Adversary — unfortunately on evidence concealed by the Church. Nor can the remarkable dermal effects produced by a Roumanian peasant girl (Eleanore Zugun) be passed over in silence, as she was intensively investigated by Harry Price and others.

The mysteries of stigmatization in their historical aspects may make us more circumspect in our evaluation of the ostensibly impressive data presented by writers like Hopkins and Strieber. Is there any firm indication of the involvement of stigmatization in Ufology? When, in 1947, Harold Chibbett experimented with hypnosis, one of his subjects was abducted to a planet where aliens caused her to be 'permanently' stigmatized.

Villas Boas's enforced sexual intercourse with the ET reduced him to the status of a stud, while even some fairly early accounts suggest the idea of genetic experimentation. It is, however, only in recent times that actual implants are mentioned; one, as we have seen, with the by-product of inducing ESP in the subject. But why, it may be asked, have they never been found by doctors and surgeons, and why are the incisions made for this purpose by the allegedly highly advanced aliens so easily detectable? Surgery on earth is sufficiently developed to avoid disfiguring scars. It can therefore be objected that such lesions as have been detected and are supposed to be proof of this are of more trivial and mundane origin and have in fact just been overlooked until such a time as they can be conveniently integrated. However, Hopkins mentions two types of scars: long, thin, scalpel-like incisions and round, deep 'scoop-marks', of which there is photographic evidence. (A photograph of a 'bullet-hole' under a girl's ear where a previous 'incarnation' had been shot dead, has recently been published and further confuses the issue.)

Hopkins makes no apology for the incompetence of his aliens, which is confounded by his statement that after one of his principal subjects, 'Kathie Davis' (Debbie Tomey) has been operated on, she became aware the next day 'that her hearing had been damaged.' In addition, 'she suffered other after-effects.' This greatly diminishes our trust in these 'superior' intelligences, whoever they may be. Still, it has to be admitted that there are indications that something very nasty is afoot and the 'all-in-the-mind' school has not got it all its own way. Psychological problems arising out of abduction experiences have reached such a pitch and have become so common in the USA that a well-meaning group of professionals under the guidance of Budd Hopkins has founded the 'Intruders Foundation', which now publishes its own bulletin.

Hopkins refers to 'bedroom visitations' that are familiar ground to psychologists and parapsychologists. The setting in these dream-like states are convincingly realistic to the experient. (This is also true of lucid dreams in which the dreamer becomes aware that he is dreaming because of inconsistencies.) In an account in Celia Green's *Lucid Dreams*, the sleeper sees nothing wrong with his environment until he tries to turn on the light. In another reported False Awakening the doctor, apparently called out at night, only notices his mistake when he starts to wash his face. In the traditional tale of the 'bedroom invader' there is either a sensation of evil and something very much amiss, or else a human-shaped phantom appears by the bedside to upset the sleeper, who is possibly in an hypnopompic state (ie on the point of awakening). The monstrosities conjured up to the sight of the abductee and the supposed physical parameters are familiar ground and can easily be assimilated even by those who like Hilary Evans stress the unsuspected powers of the subconscious.

Hopkins thinks that thousands of people may actually have been abducted without having been aware of it. In the case of Mrs Allan there are indications pointing in this direction. However, the lady in question has not been subjected to hypnosis in which people are apt to become more than usually suggestible, especially if treated by hypnotists who, like Hopkins and his associates, are firm believers in the physical reality of the abduction syndrome.

Hopkins has no wish to be abducted himself, and we can sympathize with him. It seems to be by and large a traumatic experience. We are to believe that abductions are a continuing process starting in childhood when the subject is as young as six or seven. The aliens then treat us as endangered species that have to be tagged, implanted with transmitters and carefully monitored over the years. It may be thought that so extraordinary a claim needs to be substantiated with something more convincing than mere scars, the precise purpose of which (Hopkins admits) is uncertain. Other pieces of physical evidence are equally ambiguous. Kathie Davis produced photographs of a 'circular area of ground in which all the grass appears to be dead.' Hopkins speculates that this is due to heat or radiation and akin to the familiar alleged 'landing trace' of UFOs, but Klass counters such claims by asserting that this is due to the fungal action of 'fairy rings'.

There emerges from the pages of *Intruders* and *Missing Time* a distinct and recurring type of 'Greys' with high forehead and almond-shaped eyes as portrayed on the cover of Strieber's *Communion*. With the parochialism characteristic of much of American ufology, no allowance is made for the fact that if the net is cast wider than the last few years in the USA there is no close agreement with regard to either the space-craft or their occupants. The morphological diversity is so great that it must be assumed that thousands of separate and uncorrelated journeys are made each year and that as a result of this fragmentation of effort each encounter is a single one-off affair. Alternative explanations in terms of psychology are always possible.

Abductions fail to leave unambiguous physical traces and the aliens make sure that there is no proof of their reality by not allowing us to analyse their own artefacts which are sometimes examined and even handled by abductees inside the 'craft' — unlike the Laplandic magicians who brought back some object as proof of their (ecstatic) journey. They are not independently observed, except in a single case in which it is alleged that in 1979 a Florida man, *Filiberto Cardenas*, was seen by three witnesses to have been moved from the back-seat of a car and removed to a place 16 miles distant. This took place in full view of three witnesses who were 'consciously aware and able to report it to the police.' But this is exceptional; in fact, I know of no other instance and there is certainly much to be said for the idea that encounters are one-off 'tailor made' events in which the percipients' subconscious is heavily involved. This is particularly relevant to meetings with mythological or religious entities such as Jesus, the Virgin Mary and the saints within a Christian (Catholic) context. The person thus 'visited' is assumed to benefit thereby resolving one's conflicts and fulfilling aspirations.

The psychodrama enacted at various psychological levels is beneficial and suggests that the human person involved has had the rare good fortune of being the object of divine intervention.

As in other subjects — and few are as intransigent as ufology — the writer is expected to come up with a solution; but solutions often resolve into partial explanations that fail to take into account all the relevant factors. John Spencer may well be right when at the end of his perceptive study of Perspectives he admits that 'we might have to consider the UFO phenomenon as a 'question that will never be answered''. Spencer thus considers the possibility that it *cannot* be answered.

Reverting to the suggestion that Abduction Encounters are beneficial, there is precious little to suggest this — and many indications to the contrary. At a later stage we have to consider the hypothesis that a malign power is at work. *Barney Hill*'s ulcer was thus induced. His neurosis and insomnia with nightmares lead him to seek psychiatric help.

Mr Burtoo was indifferent to the UFO landing which did not greatly affect him either way. If he was involved in a psychodrama constructed with his participation, his tale becomes less intelligible. To all appearances he happened to be in the wrong place at the wrong time. If an alien intelligence was at work, it was not of a high order!

Bob Taylor at Livingston was caught up in something over which he does not seem to have had much control and which he could easily have done without.

The three *Kentucky women* suffered ill effects, too well attested in too many cases to be ignored, while instances of healing are so rare as to be almost accidental.

The *Aveley* case is considered a lynch-pin of the theory of the beneficial psychodrama, but the data is in dispute. No doubt it did the subject no lasting harm; he greatly enjoyed the actual abduction experience, which is far from being the general rule.

The *Wotton* incident, which probably qualifies for inclusion in this study, caused nothing but terror. It took several years before Mrs Alan was able to adjust to her adventure, although her husband took it more in his stride. The MIB-like characters seen by the couple were hardly reassuring and the whole experience however, it may be classified, had not one beneficial element.

Another Surrey case, the *Spectre of Winterfold*, was also traumatic and frightening to the two young persons concerned.

It is hard to explain why M. *Cyrus* was subjected to a car accident that put him in such a shock that he was not sure whether he had survived his encounter. The after-effects were severe.

It would be interesting to know why people like Signor *Parravicini* see aliens in the first place, but presumably it did him no good and failed to solve whatever problem he may have had at the time. Another man is known to have fainted under the same stimulus. People also react unfavourably to apparitions which are psychologically induced by the subconscious according to Tyrrell's theory; but for whose benefit? Certainly not the percipient's.

The *Callery* sighting terrified a couple with its ten foot tall humanoids.

The wife of a young couple at *Piedmont*, Italy was scared by the spacemen pilots of the unearthly craft. They did not achieve much else as far as one can tell!

An ambivalent attitude is sometimes expressed by percipients of ET presences. The *schoolgirl* in Wales was finally reassured by their lack of hostility, but prefers to forget the whole thing (but is not able to). The marginally comical *Little Electrical Man* of Albany, Ohio, had a frightening stare and, although considered basically friendly, made you feel ill at ease.

The aliens seem to be aware that their activities, to say

nothing of their odd appearance, are likely to alarm their (unprepared) victims. Two Argentinians, *Juan* and *Fernando*, suffered the usual paralysis and were told not to be afraid. The whole episode does not make much sense.

A *worker* riding his moped, who did not believe in 'nonsense' like UFOs, was forcibly fed. He suffered ridicule, became totally disorientated and found the whole thing very scary.

Mrs Hingley's visitors are popular with investigators but cannot have been considered funny by the woman they inflicted their presence on. *Mrs Hingley* was affected by her visitors whom she treated with undeserved kindness, while they behaved like naughty children and caused discomfort and havoc. When she told her adventures to the public she was ridiculed.

The Finnish *forester* thought that he had been the object of an assault and was upset by his attacker. He collapsed and suffered from headaches and vomiting, and felt that he was owed state compensation.

A young farmer at *Greenburg* suffered from an acute loss of memory as the direct result of an entity sighting which affected his eyes.

Da Silva did not take kindly to an attack by masked creatures who fired at him to abduct him into a contraption which was singularly uncomfortable. Nor did he relish, or feel reassured, by the sight of corpses stacked on a shelf. The ETs finally dropped him far from home, famished and thirsty.

Travis Walton survived an unpleasant abduction ordeal. The mere sight of the UFO struck such terror into the hearts of his companions that they fled. It was not an experience to relish or to invent for amusement.

La Rubia vainly tried to escape from a terrifying craft. Blinded and paralysed like an insect, he was caught in a container. He was obliged to give up his job and his health deteriorated.

*Villas Boas'*s adventures were a mixed blessing. He subsequently suffered from conjunctivitis, nightmares and nausea.

Schirmer who had headaches, attacks of insomnia and a red welt, ceased to be a policeman.

Harrison Bailey found his energy sapped by an encounter and felt a pain in his back. He eventually became sick and aged at an unusual rate and received a disability pension.

Sandra Larson was plagued with strange dreams; her daughter was annoyed by 'presences', but at least her sinus improved dramatically.

Mr Hodges of Dapple Gray had a harrowing experience with his aliens.

Bill and *Nora* felt abject terror near Salt Lake City when they were being buzzed and were entirely drained of all energy. Seeing headless creatures was altogether too much for Nora!

PC Godfrey submitted to a terrifying experience like a walking nightmare.

A young *Venezuelan* was attacked and injured by a hairy alien.

An American *lorry-driver* fainted when attacked by a humanoid.

Two youngsters in *Maine* complained of several physical symptoms after an encounter with mushroom-shape headed aliens.

A Kentucky *truck-driver* found that his eyes had been affected after the most unpleasant experience of imprisonment in a test-tube.

A *Texas* man improved his general awareness and in his psychic faculties as the result of several episodes which are not actually claimed to have involved an abduction.

Five year old *Mary* suffered from a supposed nightmare which had psychological and physiological bad effects with severe migraine.

Ferreira, a teenager, received rough treatment from midgets in his own home.

A *Dorset* woman's hands turned red after an encounter.

A group of Cheshire *poachers* saw silvery entities and their health subsequently deteriorated.

Mrs *Verona* was treated like a laboratory animal during a 'medical'. Worse still, she was raped.

Young *Shelley McLenagham* of Bolton was very much the worse for her UFO contact, with burns, sore eyes and dizziness. Her teeth were affected.

In the 'UFO collision' at *Minnesota* there was an attack on a police car. Radiation appeared to damage the policeman's eyes, though fortunately only temporarily.

Karen was raped by 'satanic' forces during an abduction.

A *British woman* — one of a group of three — was painfully treated while told not to be afraid: the usual story.

Two *Venezuelans* were set upon by hairy entities and were thought to have been attacked by savage beasts.

Three men at *Caracas* were terrified when they were approached by giant monsters from a craft.

Llanca, an Argentinian, suffered rough handling with traumatization after being paralysed in the usual way.

Carlos Diaz had to be hospitalized after his ride in a UFO.

Corporal Valdes fainted after contact with a mysterious object. Complete amnesia set in.

A boy, *Alva*r, was knocked out by a light and forced into sexual intercourse.

A *concert pianist* and his female companion felt under attack and panicked. The woman's eyes reddened and she became ill.

Da Silva was found naked with red skin marks and an

affected area after having sex forced upon him.

Tasca had inexplicable burn marks on his back.

A New York *nurse* was raped by ETs and showed symptoms which puzzled the medical profession.

A *shop-assistant* ended up with aphasia and temporary impairment of vision. A doctor confirmed that he had suffered a severe shock.

A man from *Western Australia* began to suffer from migraine, though there was nothing medically wrong.

An *aborigine* is said to have been sucked out through a (closed) window.

An *Italian peasan*t was paralysed and robbed by midgets from an 'upturned egg'.

A *Swede* was temporarily disabled. He had burn marks on his cheek and there were psychological problems. His supposed abduction had been traumatic as revealed by hypnosis.

A *Spanish farmer* and a girl were knocked out and blinded by a hovering craft. The farmer was scared by aliens and had red marks on his cheeks.

Another *Spaniard* had his eyes affected. (Conjunctivitis is commonly reported.)

In the above extracts I have confined myself to cases already described. It seems obvious from the number of detrimental physical and psychological effects of close contact with UFOs and their purported crew that all but the most dedicated to scientific study might prefer to stay outside their sphere of influence. There are indeed one or two cases where contactees have been healed, but in the majority of instances they suffer severe shocks and traumas, though the physical effects tend to be of a temporary nature. The question is whether these are accidental, or at least unintentional, or whether a more sinister interpretation is called for.

Meanwhile it should not be thought that the idea of the 'beneficial psychodrama' is inapplicable to all encounters. In a rather unusual scenario, Nadia believed herself to be in communion with 'angeloid' beings who are wholly loving and an antidote to her depression. (She also regarded herself as a possible abductee but without evil or traumatic overtones). Rosalind Heywood, a psychic and author of books on parapsychology, when experimenting with drugs under medical supervision, similarly experienced a being that gave her 'a glimpse of what love was: infinitely far from possessive doting, quite unsentimental, yet warm and comforting — and above all personal . . .' She was literally in love with the whole universe.'

It is arguable whether such beings are subjectively or objectively perceived. Their beneficial influence on the experient is strongly asserted. This is hardly true of the grotesque and terrifying entities that snatch people from their cars or homes and treat them as objects of vivisection without any regard for their feelings.

CHAPTER ELEVEN

The discomfort generally agreed to have been suffered by contactees and abductees is negligible by comparison with Budd Hopkins's scenario as seen in *Missing Time* and *Intruders*. The central piece of the latter is the experience of 'Kathie Davis', a Mid-West housewife. Her home at Copley Woods was the centre of more than usual UFO activity. Kathie wrote to him at length, enclosing in her letter colour photographs of the supposed physical landing-site: evidence dismissed by sceptic Klass as a misinterpretation of a natural phenomenon (a 'fairy ring'). This is denied by the family, who maintain that it is not a question of fungal infestation. A more serious matter is the lesion shared by Katie and her sister. It is a long saga of contact, abduction and worse, in which the whole family participates. Spencer calls it 'perhaps one of the most thoroughly investigated cases' and has subjected it to a detailed analysis. Regarded from every point of view it is a fascinating and rather depressing story. But what do we learn from it, except not to take anything in ufology at face value?

Hopkins has found, and keeps on finding, an ever-increasing number of people who have experienced some form of abduction. They are, he says, a cross-section of the (American) population: scientists, psychiatrists, military and police officers, people in show business and the legal profession; not under-achievers or mentally ill folk. His psychiatrist consultant confirms that they do not suffer from a psycho-pathological condition, an opinion shared by Rima Laibow, MD. who also runs a support group. It has thus to be assumed that there is no known psychological cause for those cases with which she and other medical experts have been involved. Hopkins regards them as invariably harmful, although there are instances in which healing has taken place subsequent to the event.

Hopkins is an accomplished artist, but he is also a plausible and persuasive propagandist. He is too fond of questionable dilemmas of the type 'If it isn't one thing, it must be another.' Some of his data is not contemporary with the events, uncorroborated and not first-hand. His scenarios, involving implants, interbreeding with aliens and tagging, are so outrageous that, to be acceptable, they would require stronger supportive evidence. Whether or not he is always sufficiently aware of the need for the highest quality evidence is a moot point.

The main objection to his data is that it is contaminated.

When there is no obvious point of leakage — such as that which a child may have picked up from overheard conversations — there is always the possibility of thought-transference by ESP, which is particularly strong between mother and child. The evidential importance of hypnotic regression and dreams is exaggerated. In a suggestible state the subject is often subconsciously keen to please the hypnotist. Few people interested in the subject are unaware of Hopkins' strong, almost obsessive views, which he has made no effort to conceal. (Abduction, says Klass, will one day be known as 'Hopkins's Syndrome').

Dr Martin T Orne, a professor of psychiatry, is a leading authority. In his considered opinion, hypnosis so far from being the royal road to the truth, does not exclude even wilful deception by the subject and is no useful tool without independent verification. Even Freud came to the reluctant conclusion that what his patients 're-lived' was often the merest fantasy. Ufologists probing the minds of abductees for full information of their experience inadvertently pressurize them into producing false memories, so that the difference between the genuine and the imagined is not apparent even to experts, and although Hopkins has used professionals in his work, he (and others) have had 'a go' themselves for purposes of economy. The more pressure is put on the subject to remember details, the more he will obligingly supply, but with a declining ratio of reliability. If hypnosis is practised by people not totally neutral and unconcerned with the results, there is always a strong danger of the subject being 'led'. This is most likely unintentional and therefore not detected at the time. It is also desirable, for the same reason, that no outsiders should attend the sessions, a rule not invariably adhered to.

The slightest indication is accepted as proof of an abduction by its high priests: someone has had a frightening dream or he has a bad feeling on a certain road. Some of these suggestions are based on what is supposedly remembered of what happened long ago, perhaps in childhood, without making allowance for a false or defective memory. Promising subjects are probed like the witches of old and searched for physical marks on their bodies for support of this suspicion. Time Loss is considered an infallible criterion, even in the absence of an actual sighting. A professional hypnotist with much experience of the syndrome (Dr Aphrodite Clamar) is uncertain whether alleged victims of abduction have a real rather than an imagined experience. The vast majority are sincere, but so were the witches who accepted the reality of the 'witches' sabbath'.

Their persecutors meanwhile were also convinced of their ability to do harm: 'Who can enumerate the diseases inflicted', wrote the learned authors of the *Witches' Hammer* (the 16th century magistrates' manual for dealing with this supposed evil) 'such as blindness, or the sharpened pains and twistings of the body?' Black magicians thrust pins in the image representing the victim, just as witchfinders did with the real body of suspects. When this was done to Richard de Sowe by a sorcerer, the poor man progressively deteriorated in health to die within three days. (Probably due to suggestion.) The aliens thrust long needle-like instruments into the bodies of abductees to suck out an ovum. This is supposed to have happened to Betty Hill by entities who had never heard of false teeth but who posed as surgeons!

It certainly stretches one's credulity to hear that beings totally ignorant of human anatomy should be accepted as trained scientists when they conduct their so-called operations for genetic engineering, which just happens to be one of our own preoccupations at the time because of the moral dilemma posed — like the Bomb in the 'fifties during the apogee of CND. When I listened to a lecture by Budd Hopkins, I questioned him about the case of '*Sammy Desmond*', a friend of UFO investigator D. Scott Rogo. Unfortunately he was unable to comment. Rogo's well-investigated enquiry is to the point. It shows that something strange and unsavoury is happening, but something much more involved and inexplicable in human terms. Meanwhile it is wise to ignore the special pleading by proponents of the ET hypothesis that we are dealing with entities from other planets who are 'millions of years' in advance of us and whose wisdom (like God's) it is impertinent to question.

Sammy's is a long and complicated tale. (See Rogo's

Beyond Reality which, according to its subtitle, deals with the 'Role unseen dimensions play in our lives'.) As a boy, Sammy had been frightened by a bedroom-visitor. His experiences of spontaneous metal-bending predate Geller's. (There are other early instances of metal-bending.) By the time he was 30 or slightly older, he was plagued by an 'invasion of lights' in his bedroom, which were also seen by his younger sister. Much more disturbing to his peace of mind was the following event.

Sammy woke up one morning to find something like a syringe hole in his body as if a nail had been stuck in his navel and a fluid exuded from his belly button. Had Hopkins's aliens been at work? We do not have to rely solely on his word for this strange phenomenon which is confirmed by others. Next, eight midgets appeared in the backyard, climbing the fence and glowing in the dark. Eventually Sammy was subjected to a hypnotic regression by a qualified psychologist. It transpired that some 'silhouetted beings' had taken special interest in his genitals and it seemed that a long syringe-like instrument had been used on his navel. The investigation started to veer alarmingly in the direction of an abduction with the traditional 'medical'. Rogo was still more surprised at what happened to the actual tape recording of the hypnotic session. Not only was it blank, in spite of the fact that the machine worked perfectly, but it eventually disappeared altogether! Some disturbing accounts of the abduction gradually emerged, according to which the syringe that had penetrated his abdomen had been used to introduce a dark substance into his stomach. He had then been forced to watch a 'porno' film in which he was embarrassed to see that he featured himself.

The strong sexual aspects of the episode became even more explicit. His 'doctors' meanwhile had been able to relax him; instead of speaking, they just 'mumbled'. Rogo reckons that their successful relaxation technique (for which he finds parallels in other cases) was to the point in view of the distressing operation about to be carried out. Even so, Sammy panicked as they began to stick a long needle into him. Budd Hopkins, about whose subsequent work Sammy knew nothing, is wedded to the appalling concept of the removal of the subject's ovum, perhaps for purposes of genetic experimentation, (Gynaecologists consulted by him have pointed out the resemblance to surgical removal of an unfertilized egg with fibre optics). There is, of course, one snag and that is that Sammy is *male*! On the evidence before us, Sammy is to be believed. There is, then, all the more reason for caution in accepting the cruel displays of the aliens. Are they working on a belated ET Kinsey Report? Why indeed should they be interested in our sex life? It seems as if aliens have the same perverted interests as some humans.

The UFO phenomenon — and its abduction aspects — is so impenetrable that it is hardly surprising that it has given rise to some extraordinary theories once it was realised that an explanation in terms of ET entities from Outer Space was naive. This came as a shock to those looking for an easy solution:there were just too many diverse 'space-ships' with too many different crews, apparently unaware of the existence of each other. Moreover, their activities on earth were trivial and lacked scientific sophistication. They seem to mock us at every stage while posing as superior beings and Saviours of the World.

It became obvious that it was not necessary to look further than the hidden powers of the mind, whether or not we were prepared to give credence to the additional extra-sensory, psychic dimensions. Dr Vallee pointed to the realm of the fairies and came up with his own

Psychic Solution. He now thinks that something altogether more sinister is at work.

In a penetrating study entitled 'Entity or Embryo', Alvin Lawson, Professor of English at California State University, pointed out the strong physical resemblance of the standard abducting alien to the human foetus. One of the problems with abductions is that, though we refuse to take them literally as accounts describing events in the 'real' world, they are all so basically alike, including the appearance of the 'UFO surgeons' whom we have denounced as incompetent and bogus.

Lawson believes that the trauma experienced by abductees is similar to the experience of the foetus in the womb. He draws on the knowledge of a psychiatrist experienced in drug-related treatment for parallels with abduction imagery, incidentally taking issue with Berthold Schwarz's assertion that UFO-related fantasies do not occur with psychiatric patients. (Dr Schwarz is a psychiatrist who takes a great interest in the subject).

It is suggested that humanoids share many features with prenatal humans. They are usually small, with poorly developed bodies but enormous heads. Their eyes are large with rudimentary hands and feet. Their hands and feet (if any) may be claw-like and webbed. Finger- and toe-nails are often absent as are the genitals. The arms extend unnaturally to the ground, and they experience difficulties in walking. The skin is wrinkled, pallid or reddish lacking hair and eyebrows. Lawson also found 'extensive similarities between prenatal imagery and UFO abduction narratives.' Whether totally acceptable or not, the birth trauma hypothesis is of value since it can be falsified — one of the main criteria for the scientific theory — but has not lacked critics. A main objection is that it is based on an obsolete school of psychology of Rank and Grof, according to which mental imagery is the cause of neurosis and other behaviour disorders such as constipation. It was Rank who thought that the early phobias exhibited by children were influenced by memories of birth, pending on visual impressions which are later recalled with deleterious results. Of this there is no proof: the child at birth lacks any 'sense of self' of being a separate personality.

The supposed similarities between humanoids and foetus have also come under attack and are said to be disproved by the gynaecological literature. But it is when Lawson is up against the facts of collective sightings that he gets into serious trouble. He has to resort to that old stand-by, Collective Hallucination, which is unknown to psychology and psychiatry. He is also quick to dismiss the physical evidence for abductions, in stating that 'The inescapable fact is that no abduction case has thus far presented unambiguous or physiological evidence which compels us to conclude that a UFO landed in that spot, or left that mark on the abductee's skin, or abducted that family.' But some reports *do* indicate the presence of physical parameters, though the actual implications of this data are uncertain. Not all close encounters are with humanoids of the foetus-type and sometimes different types of aliens can be found together. Mrs Hingley's 'Martians' are basically fairies; others are more like frogs or apes. In this respect (and in others) they resemble apparitions which can be anything. Although most commonly in human guise, they may be no more than amorphous patches of light, clouds, shadows and mist. (Lawson confuses encounters and abductions in some discussions of entities.) Another difficulty is how to account for car-stoppages and mechanical malfunctioning, which are typically reported in connection with UFO sightings at close range.

Rites of Passage ceremonially mark that crucial stage

in a boy's life when he becomes a fully-fledged adult at the age of puberty. They have a dual aspect and function. Frightening and painful — like so many of the experiences described in these pages — they serve a well-defined sociological purpose. The child leaves childhood behind for good to be forcefully propelled into manhood. Many abductees and contactees have insisted on the incisive character of their encounter which has basically changed their outlook on life. So are the latter a psychological ploy, a psychodrama instigated by the subconscious? Perhaps so; we have an almost infinite latent capacity in this direction, as shown by the ingenuity of our dream life and the amazing visualized dramas revealed in the hypnagogic state (often confused, but by no means identical, with dreams; in this state full consciousness is retained, and the visions have a plastic quality over which we have some measure of control.) In the tribal rite a number of important privileges accrue to the neophyte in that he becomes a full member of the community with all the prospects and props of help and protection this implies. It effectively obviates the kind of identity crisis precipitated by the less formal and less embracing structure of modern 'civilized' society, in which the child is catapulted into the acceptance of full responsibility from being, as Evans so well puts it, 'a mere appendage to his parents'.

Thus both the traumatised and the assuring aspects are in evidence in both the Rite of Passage and in the abduction experience, which is none of the subject's conscious choice. An element of 'rebirth' is present in both, lending at least some plausibility to Lawson's hypothesis. There are certain concepts known to us from the studies of Shamanism like Eliade's which may well be pertinent. The symbolic 'return to the womb' is a basic ingredient of the Rite of Passage which could plausibly be incorporated in the UFO syndrome, itself 'a self-administered rite of passage'. Says Evans, 'The psychodrama of the UFO abduction is simply *the outer shell* of the experience.' (Emphasis added).

Dr Lawson's study of 'Hypnosis of Imaginary UFO Abductees,' first propounded in 1979, has also come in for criticism over the years, the latest being by Scott Rogo. Lawson attempted to gauge the degree of objective reality of those who were claiming to have been abducted. For this purpose he advertised for volunteers to be hypnotised with a minimum of 'leading'. It was assumed that his subjects were 'naive' with regard to the UFO experience, an assumption which may have been over-confident in view of the general exposure of the American public to the phenomenon.

Only 16 subjects took part in this experiment, which has never been repeated. The idea was to compare 'the genuine article' with mere flights of fancy, which may oversimplify the problem. The result was that no significant difference was found, suggesting that abduction is a 'dicey' phenomenon. There was some measure of enthusiasm for these findings among two disparate groups. One consisted of those who had become disillusioned with the ET hypothesis, the other of those who were just looking for a rational or 'natural' explanation. It seemed at last an attempt has been made to put the syndrome on a scientific footing. It is therefore all the more regrettable that Lawson's laudable project has foundered on the rocks of critical reviewing. It was this study that suggested in the first place the theory of Birth Trauma with which we are basically dissatisfied. Accepting Lawson's findings, as they were by ufologist John Rimmer, everything could be accounted for on psychological terms. Whether this is a satisfactory way of accommodating the data is uncertain. Rogo accused Dr Lawson of giving insufficient information and of 'continual use of improper experimental procedure,' as well as failure to evaluate the data properly. He is also said to have been too selective in his use of the comparative material when he should have been guarded against possible bias. Rogo points out that there are physical parameters which are not taken into account by Lawson, even if one has little belief in the 'Nuts & Bolts' theory.

The Riddle of the Men in Black is one of the most curious aspects associated with the enigma of the encounter mystery. We seem to be confronted with beings that are almost totally like us and yet lack a certain measure of reality. After a fashion, they may be thought of as having superseded the Victorian materializations of the seance room, and indeed, in common with them, they are (unlike the ufonauts) basically an *indoor* phenomenon. Who or what are these so-called MIBs? Primarily, they are imposters who pose as persons of authority like men who impersonate police officers. MIBs are a modern myth like the Phantom Hitchhiker, who *seems* to be one of us, but proves excessively elusive on closer acquaintance so as to be easily relegated to the realm of the supernatural and the delusive. They are endowed with a general degree of realism which leaves no doubt in the minds of their victims that they are indeed all they claim to be — at least at first sight.

Now this is exactly what happened in the seance-room with the phantoms conjured up by so-called physical mediums where there is room for uncertainty concerning their precise status. A Mrs Longman attended a sitting with Helen Duncan at Edinburgh. After some initial hesitation, that lady was sure that she had witnessed the sudden and unexpected manifestation of human beings to all extent and purposes indistinguishable from the sitters, except that they were temporary and fleeting structures interacting in a perfectly normal and convincing way. Yet what were these entities which apparently have no existence outside the field of experience of Mrs Longman and her friends?

There is a strange coherence about materializations which they partly share with MIBs, but in no way with most ufonauts, who present themselves in the unalluring guise of apparitional monsters of arguable probity even at a short-lived performance. MIBs are topical and play up to people's incipient paranoia and suspicion of authority especially in its covert manifestations. They falsely identify themselves as representatives of the CIA (this is largely an American phenomenon) or the MOD, but there is also a less easily defined alien dimension to them. Whereas UFO entities of the more common kind talk errant nonsense and pretend to a superior but really phoney, scientific and technical know-how, MIBs come with a clearly defined purpose to which they adhere. They seem to have some advance knowledge of an event. They are minatory yet never carry out their threats. Like apparitions, which they resemble in some way, they fall down occasionally by betraying anomalous features out of context with their affected realistic mode of behaviour.

At one level the MIBs are a modern myth, born of discontent and suspicion like modern hostility to the law enforcement agency but serve no useful function. They are part of contemporary folklore. One can draw some useful comparisons with visions of the Virgin Mary as another clearly circumscribed type of phantom. The percipient has an ambivalent conception of the configuration. The experience is, I think, like having a lucid dream which has features incorporated into it which give pause for thought and hesitation, if not for scepticism. It is an intensely personal matter which looks as if it had been carefully planned or staged by an external agency. As in abduction, proof of reality is impossible to come by. They employ an 'unnatural' process of materialization and dematerialization that is truly stunning. Adherents of Jungian psychology will regard them as 'archetypal entities' in a set of clothes appropriate to their context.

MIBs are children of their time and age, just as appearances of the Virgin fit neatly into the conceptual framework of orthodox Catholic belief, or Victorian materializations into that of the 19th century seance-room. To imply like Klass that the 'new clothes' of the MIB are the emperor's, and that there is nothing but fraudulent imitation and deception by the person who reports (no doubt mostly *bona fide*) what to him is a real and often shattering experience, is a cruel slander. (Of course, it goes without saying that there are always a few opportunists ready to cash in on a new fad.) When St. Bernardette claimed that she had seen Mary, others were accused of having jumped on the bandwagon, and when my friend in Wales encountered 'aliens' from a UFO, members of her family were suspected of having taken a cue from her. In neither case is there any proof. MIB stories run true to type with only minor variations, although we shall later discuss some more problematic cases.

The whole matter abounds in mysterious incidents and defies analysis when closely analysed. A person who has seen a UFO sometimes has not to wait long before he receives the unwelcome attention of one or more MIBs. How this is known to an outsider is puzzling when there has been no publicity. MIBs usually time their visit in such a way as to make sure that no one else is at home apart from the person they wish to warn off. They usually travel in groups of three — which agrees with UFO lore but not with apparitions, which usually appear singly. They draw up in a smart black car with fake plates to prevent later identification. They are truly 'men in black,' dressed immaculately.

The impression made on the visited person is that they are somehow connected with the secret service. They are stereotypes, both in appearance and in manner, and overawe by virtue of their supposed official status, which is never sufficiently questioned. And yet — there is something alien, or foreign about them which is enough to put one on one's guard: their skin is just a trifle too dark and their eyes a little too slantingly Oriental. And what about those reported by Hopkins that actually wore *lipstick*? But then again, does not the phenomenon mock us at *every* stage? MIBs hardly ever come over as ordinary 'human' beings: they walk stiffly like automata and betray no expression on their mask-like faces. If not overtly hostile, neither are they friendly, while their idle threats are an off-putting feature. These psychopaths are totally devoid of common humanity and retrospectively are viewed with suspicion. If checked out, they do not exist as far as the authorities are concerned in spite of occasional uniforms and other identification. They are, however, invariably well-informed, as if to render themselves more acceptable to their intended victim: in fact they are rather *too* well informed.

They indicate that they are making secret enquiries and stress that the matter should be treated as totally confidential and imply that the 'government knows all about UFOs'. Their language is based on cheap cliches of the screen and has an unnatural feel about it. Further investigation is discouraged in strong terms. Sometimes there are no actual visits but just telephone calls.

The best known case is the *Albert Bender* mystery of the 1950's. Bender 'knew' what 'it' was all about but was warned against indiscreet revelations by 'three shadowy figures' in clerical black with Homburg-style hats. Bender apparently complied with their demands to keep quiet about his inside knowledge but then published an account of the meeting! Paranoia goes well with ufology!

Other recorded instances are no less absurd. An Ohio man, *Robert Richardson*, was paid two visits by ostensible MIBs, one by two young men in a black Cadillac who questioned him about a sighting, the other by two men who arrived in a Dodge and were dressed in black and had dark complexions. They seemed to be foreign, though only one spoke with an accent. They threatened him, demanding an artifact which Richardson had picked up. It is unknown how these visitors had obtained the information, which was known to just a few people. Strangely, these implausible creatures possess paranormal powers and do not fit in with what is known of government agencies.

Dr Herbert Hopkins was a seasoned physician with an interest in the subject. Whilst on his own, he received a telephone call from the vice-president of a (nonexistent) UFO group in New Jersey. The caller made an appointment to see the doctor to discuss a current case. Dr Hopkins was surprised at the speed with which his guest arrived, especially since he did not come by car. His visitor, all in black, reminded him of an undertaker. Underneath his black hat there was no trace of hair. His skin was unnaturally white and his lips were smothered in red lipstick! In the course of an otherwise quite normal conversation he 'dematerialized' a coin in such a way that it went out of focus. Not long afterwards he complained of his 'energy running low' and experienced difficulties in moving about. He left as mysteriously as he had come, the doctor noticing a very bright light which he attributed to a UFO, though none was seen. The contrivance left some strange marks on his driveway — in a place unsuitable for parking.

There is a sequel to this story which is equally preposterous but supports in a curious way what might otherwise seem a tall tale. His daughter-in-law was contacted by phone by a stranger who claimed to know her husband. The couple had a meal with him and a very odd-looking female. They looked like robots out of gear and generally behaved in a weird manner before making an abrupt exit. The whole scene was so unreal that it only makes sense as a SF scenario.

MIBs are very much an American thing but there is the occasional British report relating to this phenomena. One came to the notice of the Manchester UFO organization and was investigated by two of its members, Peter Hough and Jenny Randles.

In 1980 *Mrs Hollins* was woken up at 2 am by a bright light from an object hovering low over some trees. It was simultaneously observed by two witnesses not far off. Hough visited Mrs Hollins who was happy to provide information but her husband, who had seen nothing, did not encourage her to talk. The sighting received passing mention in the local press, but no other publicity followed. However, a week before the investigator's visit, a man allegedly from Jodrell Bank had phoned wishing to interview her. Peter Hough was suspicious as the authorities at Jodrell Bank take no interest in ufology. It transpired that the caller had given the lady the director's name as his own. Neither of the investigators made much headway.

Mrs Hollins failed to keep appointments. (Whether or not her husband had anything to do with this is a matter of conjecture.) The whole thing was unlikely to be a hoax since the UFO had been seen by others. Mrs Hollings had perhaps been sworn to secrecy; certainly she had been put on her guard against 'cranky' people without credentials. The real candidate for this status was, of course, the MIB hoaxer himself with his bogus claim to respectability. The whole thing follows a familiar pattern particularly with regard to the MIBs false but superficially impressive cover story. Whoever he was, he was an exceptionally brazen liar, yet his deception seemed to have no purpose. The MIB syndrome is one of the most intriguing aspects of the whole UFO problem and one which we are no nearer to understanding.

One of Jenny Randles most intriguing subjects, *Shelley*, has figured earlier on. She also had mystery phone-calls and was subsequently interrogated by the dark-suited men. One, 'the Commander' was one-armed. They were supposedly experts in telepathy. During their visit they made a thorough nuisance of themselves but people appear to put up with MIBs to an unreasonable extent, perhaps because they are intimidated by their air of authority.

As mentioned earlier, *Peter* and *Sandra Taylor* from Stockport were paid a visit by two men 'from the MOD' who arrived in a black car to ask a specific question about their sighting, advising Peter not to discuss this affair.

CHAPTER TWELVE

At times it seems as if there are fashions in Ufology. Thirty years ago people saw cigar-shaped UFOs in the sky. (A barrister friend of mine came across one near Richmond.) What could one say about cigar-shaped flying saucers? Only this; that they are *out of fashion*, although UFOs have always come in all shapes and sizes. Several scholars have catalogued Ufonauts and related them to other, seemingly disparate, entities. Elves and gnomes of folklore are usually mentioned in these surveys and a few even include the Virgin Mary and Jesus.

The earliest recorded groups in modern times are the 'Aryans' reported by contactees. They are tall (1.60 m — 1.80 m), Nordic in appearance and fair-haired, though brown hair is even more common. Fair-skinned, or slightly dull skin. The head is generally exposed, but some wear helmets to go with their obligatory uniform. Exceptionally, there are females suspiciously well attuned to conditions on earth (bearing in mind that they are supposed to be ETs!). They are remarkable also for their generally non-agressive behaviour; in fact, they adopt the role of Saviours of the World as proclaimed by early contactees like *Adamski*.

Just as there is no exclusive, standard type of UFO, so there are innumerable variations in the study of the aliens and the impression conveyed by Lawson and others that they are all embryos with elongated heads and large eyes is misleading, though this type has indeed become widespread in recent times. Robots, or robot-like creatures, have made their debut. As Allan Hendry has argued, the 'coherence of data' is minimal, although he admits the existence of two 'primary groups', consisting of dwarves ('humanoid figures that range in height from 3 to 4½ feet' with 'large heads, large round eyes, long arms, and spindly bodies'), and normal-sized beings with deep eyes, but only slightly defined noses, ears and mouths. They generally wear a standard dress in the shape of an overall. The one fact that emerges is that the image is closely based or structured on *Homo Sapiens*. It should be obvious to anyone that in this respect they present an almost exact parallel to spontaneous apparitions and the psychically-induced materializations.

Ufonauts, who measure anything from several inches only to over 10 feet, defy classification when compared with specimens of the human race. 1954 yielded a rich harvest of dwarves, with a particularly large incidence in France — but not in France only! It would be interesting to know what triggered this off, when contactees have an almost unlimited choice of what may confront them. (Could one person be copying another?) Less than 20 years later, in 1973, there broke upon the ufological world the 'Year of the Humanoids'. This is the title of a study published by Professor Hynek's prestigious Centre for UFO Studies, then situated in Evanston, Illinois. Its author, David Webb, also divides ufonauts into Giants (c.7') — who are 'very ugly individuals, Men (5–6') and the ubiquitous Dwarves (c.3½') in their notorious 'divers' suits'. The giants were less favoured on the whole and in the French cases the dwarves were most frequent. But then, of course, we are talking of a country with a strong tradition of Little Folk.

Eric Zucher from France, who in 1976 (following the lead of his compatriot Vallee) drew on his vast knowledge of incidents of French dwarves throughout the ages, as seen in their rich folklore, established a connection with contemporary UFO reports. He drew up lists of a number of those entities, which included 'Lutins', a prehistoric race of industrious midgets living underground. They have a malicious streak in their nature which makes them akin to ufonauts. Their favourite dress was red and they had long blond hair. The best known variety are the Gnomes (so named by Paracelus): wise little old men from the lower regions of the earth. They traditionally associated with the fairies and even intermarried with them. It is relevant to recall that hybrid strains are deliberately encouraged by the aliens with their excessive interest in our own sexual functions. There is also the Biblical tradition of giants breeding with members of the human race in far-off times. The story of *Villas Boas*, forced to have have sex with a strange semi-human female, is a case in point.

Hailing from nearer home, but more remote in time, is the famous treatise on *The Secret Commonwealth of Elves, Fauns and Fairies*. The Scottish author, Rev. Robert Kirk, was Minister of Aberfoyle towards the end of the 17th century. His 'Secret Commonwealth' revealed the organization of the Little Folk who are said to have been ill-pleased by his indiscretion. It was widely believed that man can make a pact with them, but the precise circumstances under which this is possible are prudently concealed.

There are other people at the present time who enter into special relationships with entities. One is a young artist, *Nadia*, who felt herself surrounded by benevolent 'angeloids'; a word she invented to describe her experience. Nadia explained that these are not visions seen with the eye, but more in the nature of dreams. They are all love and very beautiful and perhaps she has even been abducted by them! Says Nadia, 'What I have seen is with my heart. Seen with my heart, they are clearer than if I could see them with my eyes. For seen with my eyes, I blink and they are gone. Seen with my heart, we are never separated. They are as lovers to one another and all are equal. They are thin and delicate, they are beautiful and there are many, though they are one being, they are a fragile creature. And they are like a field of flowers, a whole yet separate and individual. Or like a tree of flowers, but they are the blossoms, God is the tree. They are all around us, for each one of us, there is one of them, for they are us and we are them.'

It may at this point be questioned whether there can be one single answer to cover the whole field. Just as life is neither totally good nor totally bad and there is no uniformity in the human experience but great diversity, so also in the UFO enigma there are diverse and often incompatible leads in various directions.

The rare UFO that heals and the loving entities felt by Nadia are but one side of the coin; Dr Vallee and Budd Hopkins now think that they have discovered a more frightening feature of the syndrome. This will come as no great surprise to those who have followed us so far. Again and again, we have reluctantly insisted on the unpleasant character of unscrupulous 'aliens' fond of reassuring that no harm is intended. Paradoxically those who argue that our suffering at their hands is accidental are among those who most vociferously champion the (unsupported) idea of advanced ET alien technology. Its clumsiness in conducting medical examinations and in making incisions for the insertion of transplants erodes our faith in this hypothesis. Again, there is the question why these superior beings are unaware of hypnotic recall being initiated against their expressed will. These are hardly loving or caring beings; but worse was to come. When Vallee started his extended enquiry into the enigma he, in common with many of his fellow-researchers, accepted the ET hypothesis as the most economical. Dr Vallee now lives in the USA and, as we have seen, the consensus is that this is still the correct interpretation of the data. More perceptive students in Britain and on the Continent disagree.

It may well be that Vallee was never totally satisfied with the ET hypothesis, suspecting subconsciously that something did not ring true with so simplistic a notion. After all, there is no proof that there are inhabited worlds beside Planet Earth. As space-travel progressed it became apparent that the solar system is ruled out as an alternative source of intelligent life: there is no evidence that anyone is watching us from Mars (or probably anywhere else), afraid of mankind's proliferation of nuclear weapons. CND had no extra-terrestrial support outside our own communities, which have no difficulty in projecting their own apprehension onto travelling aliens from Outer Space.

Eventually Vallee, a profound and prolific writer on the subject, published *Messengers of Deceptions*. Things were evidently not what they seemed to be. But it is possible to adopt an even more pessimistic attitude when faced with the UFO invasion, and scientists have tried to disprove the idea that it does not transcend the bounds of an amusing side-show, however much the media may lampoon Little Men in Green from Mars. Is it, perhaps, deep-felt fear of this unknown occult quantity that hides behind the smiling face and the innocent chuckle?

There is yet another aspect to Vallee's lately exposed messengers: their marked *regressive* feature. (Elsewhere I have called them 'Messengers of Regression'). This is equalled by the banal utterances of mediums and their infantile romantic 'spirit controls' such as Red Indians and Egyptian princesses, not to mention the child-control 'Feda' lisping through the mediumship of Mrs Osborne-Leonard, or the little girl 'Peggy' of Mrs Duncan, who happily munched biscuits and recited nursery rhymes. The ridiculous way in which ufonauts mimic our scientific activities, dress up to impress, but talk blatant nonsense, is a comparable phenomenon. On being told what the time is, one rudely contradicts the informant. It has been implausibly suggested that there is a Zen-like wisdom in such behaviour. The MIBs in like manner adopt a superior attitude, but have failed to adapt even to the simplest mundane situation.

Take, for instance, the case of Dr *Hopkins*'s relatives who had dinner with a MIB and his 'girlfriend' after meeting them in a restaurant. Oddly enough, the young couple were wearing surprisingly old-fashioned clothes. The woman had anatomical peculiarities and both walked in an odd way as if only with difficulty. They were gawky and indiscreet in their conversation. The man was caressing his companion while openly voicing doubts as to whether he was doing it properly! It is reported that they had difficulty in moving about and were rather spooky.

Many people will be familiar with *Whitley Strieber*'s 'true story' of his persecution by alien forces as related by him in his best-selling *Communion*, which has been turned into a film. Strieber is a successful writer of SF, who (one would have thought) hardly needs the plug of a fictitious encounter to boost his book sales. Readers of his previous publications such as *The Wolfenden* will be in a better position to appreciate his peculiar psychology, which has been diagnosed as non-pathological by medical experts. There is no doubt that he was influenced by the ideas propagated by Budd Hopkins.

Strieber was terrified by weird creatures in his lonely up-state New York cabin to the point of paranoia. They did not differ materially from the grotesque figures with foetal features and large almond-shaped eyes that feature in Dr Lawson's theory of Birth Trauma, which owes its inspiration to Rites of Passage. In the film there is a happy ending in which Strieber comes to terms with his former tormentors. Few people would wish to share Strieber's experience including his one-time monitor Hopkins, who takes a grim view of alien activity. At first devastated to the point of having a nervous breakdown, Strieber found out that he was not alone in his confrontation with the inexplicable and the horrendous. His predicament was linked with the appearance in the sky of blindingly bright objects. He read about the UFO, of which he had previously been ignorant, in one of Jenny Randles's books. (It was, apparently, by mere accident that he came to read her book.) Like other contactees before and after him, Strieber is apparently wide open to psychic intrusions.

Turning to Vallee. His odyssey carried him on an apparent fool's errand through the troubled and muddy waters of ufology, starting off with the suggestion that aliens from Outer Space are visiting earth. This position became untenable long ago, though it still has its adherents. He was then struck by the psychic connection and in particular by the close parallels with tales from Magonia, that enchanted forest of earth-spirits and other mythical creatures enshrined in the annals of folklore. While these are mostly teasing rather than positively menacing (and have, anyway, practically closed up shop and gone out of business), there are other, more lethal, parameters that are less well known, propagated by writers and journalists. Strieber, by his own account, had succeeded in befriending the object of his obsessive terror, whereas others have succumbed to it.

Vallee, as a result of recent first-hand study in South America, now thinks that such experiences qualify for such adjectives as 'bizarre', 'seductive' and even 'terrifying'. The question then is, are UFOs symbols of communion and fulfilment as asserted by Strieber, or are they, on the contrary, a kind of Confrontation (the title of Vallee's latest offering)? Perhaps they fulfil different, ambiguous functions for different people, but what is their *basic* nature?

Instead of going over familiar ground and regurgitating ancient cases, the Franco-American researcher has now broken new ground by undertaking his own investigations. He enlists expert advice in many fields and uses the latest advances in photographic techniques, biological analysis and forensic science and is progressively disillusioned with the ufological fraternity who seem to be intent on proving their preconceived opinions and prejudices. (In a previous section we have shown how ufologists — especially American ones — are stuck in a rut and have got nowhere in particular.) In vain had he lectured the scientific community at large on the importance of the subject but little attention was paid to his warning. He particularly deplored the tendency to ridicule witnesses (often themselves with a good grounding in science and technology) and attempts to show them up as incapable of correct observation or interpretation — an apt illustration is the 'explanation' offered by a well-known Scottish investigator of the *Livingston* sighting. The trauma suffered by the witness, the forester Bob Taylor, was first attributed to ball-lightning. Revising his estimate of the situation a few years later, Steuart Campbell thought this may have been not ball lightning after all but an actual sighting of Venus (in daylight!). This he then thought may have triggered off a close encounter with a UFO with physical effects that included damage to his clothing.

Proceeding in a more systematic way and as the result of extensive travel to the actual sites, often in remote and inaccessible parts of the world, Vallee arrived at conclusions he found 'terribly disturbing' and frightening. Twelve cases involved fatalities within a very short space of time (2 days or less).

CHAPTER THIRTEEN

Most people in modern times dismiss the more frightening aspects of ufology and witchcraft as superstition. What are the facts about witchcraft? It is no doubt true that most so-called witches of the 16th and 17th centuries, when the witchcraft persecution was raging most fiercely, were poor and starving old women, more eccentric than dangerous. Most would nowadays be diagnosed as mentally ill. There were people who believed they could do evil.

Those two notorious witch-hunters of the sixteenth century, Springer and Kramer, complained bitterly of there being no end to the evil deeds attributed to and confessed by their victims, conveniently ignoring their own mindless cruelty; 'Who can enumerate the diseases inflicted, such as blindness, or the sharpened pains and twistings of the body?'.

A contemporary French writer (Cardan) depicts witches as 'deformed, bloodless and somewhat dark . . . taciturn and foolish, differing little from those possessed by demons'. There was, Cardan fancied, nothing wrong with them that a square meal would not have put right. The fact remained that less charitable folk persistently alleged that their evil nature was only too clearly reflected in their debased physiognomy. Such people readily accepted the popular belief that they had much in common with vampires in causing the death of innocent persons. The legal charge against them was one of 'malice' or *maleficium*.

To quote but a few examples of supposed malice in action. In 1326, ie in a period much earlier than that in which the Witchcraft craze was to flourish, one Robert le Mareschal was hanged for conducting a drastic experiment in the Black Arts. Robert had thrust a pin into an image of Richard de Sowe with the result that the latter progressively deteriorated in health, lost his reason and then died within three days.

Frau Blanckenstein was the daughter of a reputed witch, which made her a target for suspicion. She was visited by a soldier who, by order of Council, was to levy poll-tax on her property. Straightaway this unwelcome visitor's eye began to swell yet, having remonstrated with her, he was cured the next day as confirmed by another soldier. Shades of the temporary conjunctivitis inflicted by ufonauts? In the 19th century Jules Bois, as the result of occult experiments claimed to have been successful, became convinced of the effectiveness of Black Magic, while the learned authors of the *Witches' Hammer* were equally sure from their experiences that they 'suffered intolerable assaults, specially at night' in this case because of their strong stand against witchcraft.

Centuries pass by, and the *maleficium* complained of in past eras is still part and parcel of the incubus syndrome. A young man hexes a rival for a girl's affection so that he is nearly killed, suffering from feelings of nocturnal strangulation. Sir Richard Rainsford postulated the existence of 'involuntary witches' who harm their own property, while some ufologists argue that any injury done to contactees and abductees is unintentional — a theory at variance with their trust in the superiority of these beings. It is consistent with the idea of uncontrolled psychic powers working via the victim's subconscious mind. The idea of *maleficium* was defined within the context of contemporary belief-systems as ' ... a vicious act entered into with the witch, through the assistance of some person satisfying his own malice.' (Vallee's update is in terms of a sinister alien technology.)

Paranoia ruled supreme when manuals like the *Witches' Hammer* were as popular with magistrates as Stone's is today and even acts of ostensible kindness such as making presents were looked at askance: what mother would allow her child to accept an apple from an old hag? Nor is it advisable to take food and drink from an alien and — possibly — aliens are as wary of eating and drinking our own staple nourishment. We have seen earlier that the evidence for aliens consuming our food is ambiguous. Eating fairy food invariably leads to dire consequences!

Accusations could not always be accepted at face value. At Frankfurt a woman confessed to the murder of children, but their parents knew that they had died of normal causes, while some victims of supposed lethal sorcery were actually still alive. There were other suspicious aspects of this subject. A Devonshire woman, Alice Butler, was 'examined' in 1601. A fisherman of the same county had been put on a serious charge. He had predicted, or threatened, that Alice's child was going to suffer from a lack of vitality, there being apparently no signs of ill health. Seventeen weeks later the child fell sick and died. The fisherman and his wife had a local reputation for witchcraft. It seems that such cases were not rare.

Mother Munnings, a precursor of that modern genus, the sitting tenant, could, it is alleged, only be dislodged by strong-arm tactics. When her landlord finally resorted to such methods and physically removed her front door, her threat left nothing to the imagination: 'Go thy way, thy nose shall lie upwards in the churchyard before Saturday next!' No sooner said than done; the poor man falls ill on the Monday, dies on Tuesday, and is duly buried that very same week. (Luckily for the the woman, that great champion of the oppressed, Sir John Holt, acquitted her.) During the Commonwealth, a would-be eradicator of all wickedness and zealous collaborator of the Witchfinder General, Hopkins, was impressed by the curse of a 'very aged man' to the effect that a neighbour's tongue should 'rot'. Alas, the curse took root.

Michele Soppe flourished towards the middle of the seventeenth century. He was a man of many useful talents, for not only could he control the weather, but he was also able to 'hurt anyone he wanted ... and make them sick, wither and die.'

The unedifying tale of the weaver Andrew Ardes and his kin can be summarized as follows and, as usual with accounts of this type, it raises more problems than it solves. A particularly touchy shrew, Janet Wisehart, was teased by Ardes in what might be thought a playful manner. Flying into a towering rage disproportionate to the supposed offence given, but not out of character, she predicted or threatened that he was to survive less than a month to provide for his bairns. Another month passed, and his wife was no more. Ardes himself fell ill almost at once and passed over within the span of one week. As a result of this double tragedy the children were reduced to begging for bread.

The cattle mutilations attributed to the UFO occupants are controversial, but some experts while not keen to get involved in this aspect, take them seriously. Witches were credited with inflicting harm on farm animals and of killing them. There is a pamphlet describing the *Condemnation and Execution* of Anne Foster in 1674. Displeased by a grazier's curt refusal to sell her some mutton (and to be fair to the man, such intercourse with a witch was considered a hazardous business) she was heard to mutter curses. Within a short time, whether by sheer coincidence or otherwise, thirty of his sheep were dead, 'their bones all shattered in their skins.' A month later there was an unexplained and mysterious conflagration in which he lost his house and barns. Anne confessed to both crimes, even threatening further outrages. She was chained to a post in gaol and ultimately suffered death by hanging, the legal punishment for sorcery in England.

William Perkins, a distinguished Cambridge divine, made his name with a *Discourse of the Damned Art of Witchcraft* (1608). Although he maintained that the powers attributed to witches were imaginary and that they were deluded melancholics, he believed that they could perform acts of malice like killing cattle at a distance with the Devil's aid.

Parapsychology knows a phenomenon called 'Stallspuk' (almost totally confined to the Continent) in which stabled animals are afflicted at night and suffer contortions. Dangerous 'beams' are complained of in other contexts. A Jamaican woman living in Thornton Heath told me that she was continually harassed at night by a next-door neighbour; a compatriot and a teacher. The harmful, noisy rays sent through the walls of the house prevented her from sleeping. Her story was not confirmed by her tape recordings or by investigation. Is it a coincidence that the infliction of scars and other lesions has lately been reported independently and without any obvious connection in cases of (a) Reincarnation; (b) contact with UFOs; (c) mediumistic manipulation? In the latter instance it has been demonstrated in a laboratory that the heart can be slowed down and stopped by 'psychic' powers.

As regards (a), not all amount to 'congenital deformities or birthmarks', though a high proportion no doubt do. The evidence for (b) is mainly supplied by Budd Hopkins, and has already been discussed. Dr R M Neal in his 'Medical Injury Protocol' investigated anomalous physiological effects on humans through contact with UFOs, including healing and 'parapsychological activity.' Also at issue are possible psychosomatic discomforts suffered by people in close contact alongside permanently deleterious effects like skin-lesions, gastrointestinal disturbances and similar pathological manifestations. Among the more disturbing ones is the Cash-Ladrum incident, where radiation-like symptoms affected the witnesses for a prolonged period of time. (c) Most suggestive of the mediaeval concept of *maleficium* was the ability of the Leningrad housewife *Nina Kulagina* to induce burns on the skin, to slow down and stop the heart of animals and men, as well as to heal the sick.

In a case recently investigated by Vallee it was found that the spots on an alleged victim's back could be accounted for by insect bites and scratches, as they bore no resemblance to puncture-marks; which only goes to show that one cannot be too careful in the evaluation of anomalous evidence. My belief in the phenomena of Madame Kulagina is based on first-hand data and meeting her chief investigator Dr Sergeyev on my visits to the Soviet Union.

Mrs Victor, a Californian, is a contactee who has seen aliens wearing the usual silver suits. Following a reported contact she was assaulted by invisible entities who threw her to the floor, beat her violently and broke her leg. Parallel accounts exist of the saints such as the French mystic, *Thérèse Noblet*. The suffering and humiliations of *St. John Baptist Vianney*, known as the Curé d'Ars, make unpleasant reading because of their unsavoury connotations. In an old account of strange happenings on a highway near Emmerich in Germany, it is recorded that travellers were constantly beset, beaten, thrown off their horses, their vehicles overturned etc. While all this was happening, only a hand could be seen. Readers will be relieved to hear of the happy end: when a witch was burnt at the stake, there was no more trouble at the spot!

I have seen a heavy and disabled man pushed from behind in such a way that I was afraid he was going to land on me, but the fall was broken at the last moment. He had recently suffered injuries to body and clothes when in attempting an exorcism he unleashed still more violent forces, powerful enough to buckle a heavy metal door.

Dr. Vallee chronicles perplexing goings on in remote parts of South America. He paid a visit to the site of the death of two men who had been found lying side-by-side on the top of a mountain at Rio de Janeiro. The whole thing pointed to a connection with a UFO cult, though the clues were ambiguous. As the result of his enquiries Vallee now no longer believes that the phenomenon is either quaint, beneficent or just trivial. Something is going on that suggests a 'superb, advanced technology'.

Modern weapons perfected by man with the intention to disable could be lethal, pending on their range: so have we been anticipated by this alien technology whose motivation we fail to understand? Is ufology witchcraft in an up-to-date guise? Many of the phenomena studied by ufologists as if something new and unheard-of turn out, on close inspection, to be old 'friends' unfortunately not at all like the earlier manifestations of handsome alien Saviours from the sky.

If a government cover-up is more than a paranoid fantasy by people intent on knocking the authorities, it would involve this particular worrying dimension of the UFO enchantment and not just the general question of whether or not 'flying saucers' really exist.

A similar parallel could be established with Old Witchcraft — not the spurious modern revival of a surviving fertility cult but with the 'real thing' chronicled in the annals of the sixteenth and seventeenth centuries when, among generally pervading superstition and ignorance of psychology, there was also the realisation that something was basically wrong.

There is some kind of pattern in the chronological sequence of events. This relates to progress from the threat or curse by the witch (*damnum minatum*) to its supposed ultimate effect (*damnum secutum*). There is some uncertainty as to which came first: the actual injury (as hard data) or the bewitchment or *envoûtement* by an ill-disposed person or persons. The question therefore arises (but is beyond the competence of the present enquiry) whether witches, — who duplicate many of the miracles of their godly counterparts in addition to working evil, — suffered undeservedly as a class, which is arguable on the evidence.

Van Dassel expressed the opinion that ' . . . the judge cannot err in repeating torture, for witches seem not to have been sufficiently tortured.' This was in 16th century Europe, where the rack was not only legal as part of the 'examination', but encouraged, though a few brave souls spoke out against it. There was an ultimate revulsion against the whole concept of *maleficium* when it came to be realized that confession was wrung from the victims by barbaric means, unlikely to reveal the truth. This did not apply so much to England, where torture was illegal, though rough treatment of the accused was not unknown.

Closer to our own time Jules Bois, writing on the 'Bewitchment of Hate' in his great study of Satanism and Magic, accepted the reality of *envoûtement* (enchantment) by referring to certain experiments by his fellow-countryman de Rochas, while Nandor Fodor, a Freudian analyst and noted psychical researcher, 'had personally known several people who *claimed* the possession of demonic power that made people drop dead.' (My emphasis). Fodor was a believer in 'malign telepathy', which does not figure large in the parapsychological literature. But even at an early time there were many cases of sudden death which an admittedly superstitious culture did not relate to arcane causes. Granted that the accused person was guilty as charged of evil intent (which is far from certain in many instances where the supposed witch was a crazy, starved old biddy), one would have to be satisfied of its *effectiveness*. Bodin made a surprising attempt to come up with an answer at a statistical level and arrived at a cautious verdict, but as usual opinion was divided and the contemporary Jeanne of Montenaie (in 1582), boasted that her own form of sorcery was nearly always instantaneously effective.

Macfarlane who, more than any other student of witchcraft, addressed himself to the problem of paranormal involvement, provides a breakdown for the study of this parameter. His book states the 'Duration of illness ascribed to witches in Essex Assize indictments' covering the period 1560–1580. It deals with accusations of having caused death following sickness lasting *from one week to three months*. There is a steady decline in the victim until three years have elapsed, when there are only residual instances of lingering disease but without related fatalities. Records of sudden disaster as the result of a curse or foresight as in the Bible (e.g. Pelatiach; Ezek.xi,13; Ezekiel's wife: Ezek.xxiv,15) are uncommon, but not unattested: Mary Lynn, who had a grievance against a widow 'wished the pox to light upon her.' Within a few hours (and perhaps due to the power of suggestion), a 'sudden weakness' befell the latter, accompanied by psychokinetic phenomena. No particular diagnosed ailment is mentioned; often it is its unexpected nature rather than the illness itself that gave rise to suspicion of foul play. The basic theory is that the indulgence in acts of malice results in selective affliction of body or mind (or both), often with a fatal outcome.

Compared with the phenomena of ufology, the philosophy of witchcraft seems simplistic almost as if to illustrate Occam's famous dictum that the most uncomplicated explanation is always to be preferred; which drove Bunge to protest against this 'razor' that he would rather be hairy and alive than shorn to the skin and dead. It was not that every misfortune was then attributed to evil intent. Some accusations (and it seems that people felt free to accuse others regardless of the consequences) were discovered to be baseless, as when the 'victim's' parent testified that their child's demise had been due to natural causes, or that he was still alive! Similarly exponents of tribal philosophy almost universally blame disasters and death on supernatural agencies, but are divided in their opinion with regard to what is actually due to witchcraft and sorcery and what portion of it must be assigned to alternative causes. To revert to Macfarlane, death by witchcraft occurs frequently within a single week, though not as commonly as within a more protracted time-lag of one to three. In the medieval case of de Sowe quoted earlier on, it will be remembered how he 'immediately became frenzied' when a pin was inserted into the head of a magical image to succumb within three days after it was driven into its heart.

With UFOs there appears to be something infinitely more powerful. 'Progress' has had its way in this as in every other field! Witches worked only at close quarters. The historian noted that the Essex witches (about whom we are particularly well informed) operated over a limited range, so that it was found expedient to banish them to remote parts of the country where their powers were neutralized by the intervening distance.

Most Parapsychologists also are aware of the fact that psychokinesis is most effective over a limited range. As to the supposedly ultra-modern appliances of the ufonauts, we know practically nothing. Time and time again we hear of UFOs zooming in on their victims, while ufonauts sport 'SF' space-guns with which they immobilize at short range the approaching over-curious. In the case of Mrs Hingley they do not even have this dubious excuse to fall back upon, rather they wilfully and sadistically inflict their technology on a defenceless woman who offers them hospitality.

To the best of our knowledge we have done nothing to offend these grotesque monsters who have taken it on themselves to invade our living-space. The down-trodden witch, who put a burden on the village economy, but who might be refused a handful of cherries from a local vicar, had good reason to be the aggrieved party and to vow vengeance on the mean incumbent; but what of the lady from Warwickshire who was minding her own business at home and moreover comes over as a kindly and generous soul?

There is an anecdote about the famous Scottish medium D.D. Home according to which he dislodged a 'sitting tenant' by causing poltergeist phenomena in his home. A reprehensible abuse of psychic powers, perhaps, but Home was doing it to oblige a friend who may have had good reasons. And what, in the long run, did Mrs Hingley's tormentors achieve apart from providing us with interesting material for our book? For, alas, we are no nearer to understanding tales of this kind. It is of little help to be told that these 'advanced' entities are beyond our comprehension, which is indeed so. On the other hand, their behaviour does not suggest that they are endowed with any kind of superior rational or moral brain; they act like poltergeists that play childishly annoying tricks and just occasionally do serious harm to humans. When I was freely moving around in a haunted garden-shed (investigating the Bromley poltergeist case), I was not afraid of the heavy weights that flew round the premises, since I knew, as everyone knows, that poltergeists never attack physically. Then what about the main character, poor Mr *Elms* with his arm in a sling? Not only had he lost his jacket with all his holiday money but, attempting an exorcism according to some secret esoteric rite, he had been injured. A saw had been rammed down his back and he complained of violent physical effects on his shed.

This is therefore another field where people labour under the misconception that it is a relatively trivial matter without peril to mind, life and limb. Vallee has tried hard and unsuccessfully to disabuse scholars of this dangerously misleading misconception. He has of late begun to concentrate on what he calls the 'clinical data': the UFO impact on the witnesses apart from that on the environment. He draws attention to the fact that M. *Masse* of Valensole was afflicted, like many others who had been in close contact with the phenomenon, by temporary paralysis that continued to affect him for some time after the actual sighting. Mr *Elms* was pushed hard from behind in my presence while Mr *Flynn* in Florida nearly collapsed through the draught produced by a landed saucer and was unconscious for a day. Almost blind, with a dark spot on his head, he became deaf and felt numb. Radiation-like effects are commonly complained of, while one particularly unfortunate man found that his skin was peeling.

There is a certain ufologist whose ambition is to kick the tyres of an ET craft to satisfy himself of its physical presence. Apart from being naive in seeking such ambiguous proof, he could also endanger himself! A prospector for minerals wearing a rubber-coated glove did actually touch the surface of a craft to see his glove melt and his shirt catch fire. His subsequent physical sufferings were extensive. A Scottish poltergeist case, by contrast, included symptoms of ostensible possession. This is rare in this context and practically unheard of. UFOs present themselves as machines of solid aspect but not invariably; contrast the transparent configuration from the sky whose components and attachments (somewhat resembling mines) attacked a forester at Livingstone (also in Scotland).

The north-country teenager, *Shelley McLenagham*, had purple rashes as the result of a close encounter near Bolton. She had a pain in her eyes and joints with serious damage to her teeth, which partially disintegrated. It was reported during the Korean War that an entire artillery unit became ill as a result of the descent of an orange-coloured luminous object and were unfit to carry out their duties. Probably no single explanation can account for everything, both magnetic fields and pulsed microwaves having been suggested. A particular sinister development of the most dangerous type seems to be confined to inaccessible parts of Brazil. These are the so-called *chupas*, box-like objects with powerful searchlights flying at night. They hum like refrigerators, or transformers, with lights at either extremity and are relatively small; presumably drones, as they are too little to contain a human being. Several people, usually night-time game hunters, have fallen victims to them.

One suffered for three days before finally succumbing to these beams, having gone mad with sheer terror. The light is bright enough to light up the whole area. Official confirmation is hard to obtain, but the data are well established. These are no mere accidents: the victims who are deer hunters are being hunted themselves.

Yet it is difficult to believe that whatever sends the *chupas* on their mysterious mission is hostile to the human race as such.

There are many aspects of the UFO enigma which are inexplicable on current scientific theory. Among these we may mention the power to materialize and dematerialize instantly like psychic structures, as well as the phenomenon of 'matter-through-matter' (demonstrated to Crookes). Dynamic shape-shifting and merging also occur. 'They' have the ability of stopping us recording the phenomenon in action; people armed with cameras have been unable to operate them, or have been 'persuaded' of the uselessness of the exercise as if 'they' did not wish us to confirm the fact that there are real physical parameters. This also accounts for the absence of totally convincing evidence. The best is, as with the Yeti, the footprints (and impressions of landed craft). Occasionally abductees have either taken artifacts, or even been given them as mementos, but not in a single instance have they been permitted to keep them for analysis. A typical example is a lady who was at first allowed to take something as proof, but was disappointed when permission to keep this vital piece of evidence was withdrawn.

Abductees desire corroborative proof of the (physical) reality of their experience, as they are likely to be disbelieved or even ridiculed; some have found it expedient to keep quiet for years, telling no one. If you were to experience a UFO encounter, would you confide in others if you had always discounted such possibilities? What is strange is that there are many cases where people almost succeeded in getting proof, only to be finally frustrated. But what would you reasonably expect from those in charge of a structure which, according to one account at least, is actually larger inside than outside or a flying object made of stone?

Abduction reports also fail to make sense as they vary drastically depending on the hypnotist involved. Dr Sprinkle's subjects are happy, whereas Hopkins's are not, and Klass gives some good (though perhaps tongue-in-cheek!) advice to go to Leo Sprinkle for your hypnotic regression rather than to Hopkins and his followers for a 'good trip' to meet 'nice' ufonauts. It is certainly strange as Hopkins is a pleasant and kind man. Or is it just a question of expectation, brought to the surface by suggestion, unconscious prompting, or even cognitive resonance as suggested by the researches of Rupert Shelldrake in another field? Hypnotic regression, habitually carried out by unqualified amateurs unaware of the pitfalls is, in Klass's well-chosen book-title 'A Dangerous Game', while lie-detector tests, much favoured in the USA, are a dubious tool as they are easily outwitted.

If abductions are all fantasy and fraud as assumed by Klass, there still remains the obscure factor of the physical parameters. As Vallee discovered in his attempt to secure first-hand evidence from remote parts of the world, this is no easy matter. We are referring to the deadly *chupas* of the Brazilian jungle in regions far removed from hospitals and the most elementary medical care. The case of the hunter *Ramon* is typically frustrating in view of the effort made to interview first-hand witnesses. Did he die of a heart attack? The evidence is against it. Ramon was only forty at the time of his death and in good health with no record of cardiac trouble. He had been out at night hunting and gone to sleep in a tree. Before he set out his family had warned him, but Ramon laughed at their fears. The main reasons for thinking that he had fallen victim to an attack of which he died soon afterwards, are: his previous good health, with no indications of an heart condition; the prevalence of *chupas* in the area at that time; the presence of red marks below the ear.

None of this is conclusive and unfortunately permission for an inquest was refused by the family. If this were the only record of this kind there would be room for more doubt and readers are referred to Vallee's *Confrontations* for further evidence. It is sobering thought; and why is the phenomenon in its extreme form apparently confined to a particular region?

Drawing on still further mysteries, it is one thing to ask questions, but quite another to answer them. Jacques Vallee, who over the years has done much to try and elucidate this ultimate enigma, came up with a 'Psychic Solution' in 1977. But what kind of 'solution' did he have to offer? UFOs, he found, were neither to be dismissed as some kind of mass-hypnosis, nor were they 'agents from some alien intelligence' but, much more dramatically, 'mirrors of a psychic reality originating in the human consciousness to serve and perhaps guide man's need for the future'. Did it actually solve all the problems of this elusive phenomenon? Like most of us, he had at first been inclined to follow the ufological 'party-line' in thinking in terms of something mechanical from beyond Planet Earth. But where precisely from? This was the big unanswered and unanswerable question.

While others failed to progress beyond the deceptively convenient let-out of Flying Saucers 'from out there', Vallee noted the many unmistakable parallels with Magonia, the fairyland of myth and folklore. Andrew Lang had pointed out the similarity between it and many of the paranormal mysteries studied by the Society for Psychical Research which had been hitherto generally ignored. Vallee fared little better: the fact that abductions in particular were nothing new was not a welcome discovery to the likes of Hopkins. They attempted to defuse the situation by referring to a 'folklore of obviously uncertain authenticity.' The reverse action was that of some European scholars, who concluded that all talk of UFOs and abductions could be dismissed as unfounded in 'real' experience. Both are extreme positions which have to be rejected as valid objections to the massive testimony by basically honest and reliable people all over the world — and indeed throughout the ages. Meanwhile, are we any nearer to a real solution?

Is the UFO phenomenon all of one piece, or is it diverse? Is there any necessary connection with coloured lights that harm no one and seen and photographed in inaccessible parts of Norway and the *chupas* of remote regions of Brazil which one witness describes as 'the most beautiful thing she had ever witnessed'? Photographic and other evidence negates assumptions such that the witnesses were simply hallucinating. Was *Dr Carvalho* right about the monstrosities that caused so much suffering and death to her compatriots?

Another deadly enigma, this time not admired by anyone, is Spontaneous Combustion; the Fire that comes down from Heaven. Old Testament prophets are said to have invoked it successfully against the worshippers of false gods. Everyone knows how Elijah challenged the priest of Baal on Mt. Carmel and how their frenzied self-immolation proved singularly ineffective. The man of God then built an altar, surrounded it with water, pouring water on both the sacrificial animal and the firewood, whereupon after an appropriate invocation to Yahweh, the fire of the Lord fell and consumed the burnt-offering, the wood, stones and the dust. Legendary though this account may be, and it has been questioned where all the water came from during a period of severe drought, the theme of Fire from Heaven runs through much of biblical literature and is also of significance to shamanistic tenets in which it figures as basic to the cosmos itself as well as to cultic ceremony.

Even more relevant than Elijah's victory over Baal is the story of how he disposed of the luckless 'captains of fifty' sent to arrest him by royal command. The officers found him majestically sitting on a hilltop wearing his professional garb of hairy garment, a leather girdle round his loins and pronouncing a virtual death-sentence on his apostate sovereign, King Ahaziah of Israel. Fire from Heaven consumes the soldiers for daring to lay hands on the holy man.

There is evidence for miracles in our own time which points to an unknown power no less lethal, than the South American *chupa*. This is Spontaneous Human Combustion (SHC) without an ascertainable cause which, though well-attested, is fortunately rare. Its result is the almost complete incineration of the human body by selective flame that spares the victim's clothes together with most of the furniture. This sometimes happens without the presence of a normal fire, as in the middle of a dance-floor. *Chupas*, SHC: these are the extremes of perilous contact with the Unknown, call it UFO phenomenon, Flying Saucer, or simply the Paranormal. But as we have seen, other less traumatic aspects have to be taken into consideration. Healing has in some cases been associated with UFO contact; but on balance it would appear that it is to be avoided rather than sought out for one's own good. Extraordinary recoveries from incurable diseases are part and parcel of the religious domain and the power of the human mind is often underestimated.

Guy Lyon Playfair wrote of the 'impossible' cure, by hypnosis, of a rare skin disease. The no less incredible sequel is of equal importance in the elucidation of this feat. When the young doctor who had achieved this came to realise that crocodile skin is allegedly 'incurable' he was no longer able to help other patients suffering from the same complaint!

Some scholars believe that Abductions are only 'in the mind', although initiated by an external stimulus. The exact nature of this stimulus is obscure and we have expressed scepticism about the assumption that Mr *Bob Taylor* entered the Dimensions of Enchantment because he saw an invisible planet. This is not to say that misperceptions and illusions of various kinds of stimuli such as bright stars and 'space junk' are irrelevant. Many experiences involving close encounters with resulting abduction scenarios take place at night when the subject is under the influence of a fatiguing and monotonous activity. For some reason the subject is startled by the sight of what may be a prosaic celestial object, natural or man-made, and subsequently catapulted into an altered state of consciousness not shared by bystanders who may afterwards report nothing out of the way. Thus in a famous Australian case only one person entered an alternative dimension to the surprise of a ufologist who was in the same car. Very exceptionally there is independent corroboration of the whole or, more usually, part of the abduction experience. This does not mean, that there is no substance to the account, a negative conclusion convincingly negated by the hard data, which have already been summarized, with a powerful boost by Vallee's latest investigations.

As to the entities, they also present a serious problem, although we can place them alongside such well-known phenomena as apparitions, spirits, impersonations of religious figures or of our dear departed. These shape-shifting configurations are masters of deception and adapt themselves like modelling clay to our cultural milieu and belief-structures, being alternatively, beneficent and reassuring or menacing and evil. At best, they reflect popular current ideas on 'green' issues, at their worst, they talk incoherent rubbish and go in for that kind of pseudo-scientific jargon which is a mere projection from the percipient's immature mind. Are these then so many insoluble enigmas? It does at times indeed look that way; at present we do not even know how ESP works, while many scholars deny its very existence and some similarly fly into the face of massive evidence to proclaim their disbelief in the existence of UFOs — not to mention their more exotic parameters.

It would be helpful to be able to point the reader to firm conclusions but these are few and far between. There is much speculation by armchair critics, but a number of good studies of the subject have been published of late. Some of the best are less well known than they deserve to be in this country as they are in French or Spanish. Among English authors John Rimmer, a librarian in Surrey, who publishes the magazine *Magonia*, lays stress on the fact that accounts of abductions are personal to the experient and strongly influenced by his own life and experiences. At the same time, their underlying symbolism supplies a strong emotional element. Again, Rimmer insists, and insists rightly, on the continuum with ancient legend, while at the same time they are firmly grounded in present-day problems and preoccupations. Based on these findings, he concludes that 'the abduction experience is almost totally psychological in origin', rejecting as unsupported by fact the ET hypothesis just as we ourselves have been forced to do. On the other hand, it may be thought that too much importance is attached by him to the Birth Trauma Hypothesis. Abduction reports, Rimmer confirms, are 'important' in containing a message about ourselves and the kind of world we live in, 'even if that message comes from within ourselves'.

As we have seen, the psychological approach does not satisfy Budd Hopkins and his followers in America. They attempt to disprove it by getting a psychologist to conduct a successful test experiment, which seemed to be reinforced by Eddie Bullard's discovery of what he called 'doorway amnesia'. It was found that when people simply tried to visualize an abduction, they naturally entered the craft by its door, whereas in 'real' cases hardly anybody ever mentions how they got inside: one minute they are outside, the next they describe the interior without mentioning how they gained access.

Jenny Randles considers the possibility of 'time-travel', a concept deriving from (and perhaps best left to) science fiction. Now it has been shown that many of the salient features of the syndrome have been surprisingly anticipated by the latter, indicating that Nature indeed imitates Fiction. However, time-travel goes a long way way beyond this and is a fantasy about people travelling backwards in time from the future, perhaps with the object of warning us humans about the errors of our ways — after the catastrophe has already happened! Ufologists cannot be accused of lacking in imagination.

It does not look that Randles takes time-travel too seriously as a plausible scenario and the warnings of imminent global disaster are explicable as percolations of various strongly held view and anxieties. She is, however, at pains to dispel the fallacy of the ET intervention into our world affairs by superior beings of undisclosed origin, still less is she inclined to accept the chilling 'data' for implants by these aliens. 'Interspecies fertilization' is the name of their supposed game, with the object of creating hybrid creatures able to live 'here and there'. I do not care for them as a species and do not believe in this bizarre and totally unacceptable idea. Nor can I put much trust in Persinger's all-embracing explanation by transients of temporary columns of radiation from and into the atmosphere, since his data do not check out too well. What I do believe is that the UFO problem with its associated subdivisions will be with us for a long time both to fascinate and puzzle and even to terrify. People demand an answer from those who pass as experts and are unhappy if there is none. The recent history of the corn circles is a case in point, where people have been unduly impressed by 'scientific solutions' that fail to solve, but 'look good.' This is also true of Persinger's theory and of the late Guy Lambert's attempt to solve the poltergeist enigma in terms of seismic and underground water influences on unstable domestic structures.

There is something real and substantial out there, whether physical or semi-physical, which we do not understand — and may never fully understand. After more than a hundred years of intensive study by the Society for Psychical Research and others we still discuss *the evidence for* ESP! Nor can we be certain even now why some people see UFOs, aliens and apparitions, while others do not and cloak their ignorance with scepticism or worse still: denial of the facts.

In his last published book prior to his untimely death Scott Rogo postulated a 'secret language' operating in the abduction experience whose hidden messages and symbols are hard to uncode as insufficient information is so often given about the experient himself.

In this country Ken Phillips of BUFORA has engaged on an extensive programme of 'Anamnesis' in collaboration with Alex Keul, an Austrian psychologist. This project explores the psychological profiles of the witnesses and common parameter of their lives. Phillips found that they tend to be discontents and loners who have more than usual paranormal experiences. This did not come as a surprise, as ESP and out-of-the-body journeys are frequently reported in connection with close encounters and abductions. On the other hand, it appears that sightings of UFOs are not the privilege of any type of person, but are common property. In this context we may recall the frequent allegations of extensive communication with the ufonauts via 'telepathy', which is not attested elsewhere. On the other hand, so-called out-of-the-body travel (or 'astral' travel) is a relatively common (and not necessarily psychic) phenomenon akin to lucid dreaming, when the dreamer has doubts about the objective nature of what is happening in sleep at the time because of certain recognized inconsistencies with his waking life.

OBEs have many features in common with the abduction experience like passing through a tunnel and seeing a bright light, and the literature of the subject is extensive. Some, like Blackmore, favour a purely 'natural' or psychological theory, while others postulate a paranormal element on the basis of their own experience which has also been found in Near Death accounts. It is therefore clear that psychology (and parapsychology) must play an important part in any attempted elucidation of the enigmas under discussion, involving many disciplines, including physiology and medical expertise. Their inherent intransigence is shared with other anomalies, particularly the study of entities and the all-too-physical poltergeist, traditionally and etymologically a boisterous spirit but now considered to be a force inherent in the human psyche. It almost seems at times as if there are phenomena which become more obscure and inexplicable the more they are studied; abductions and their related concomitants are prime candidates.

As John Spencer puts it, 'If UFOs are extra-terrestrial then that will be possibly the most important and significant event ever to have occurred to mankind.' He entertains serious doubts about the validity of this still undeservedly popular theory. His own 'radical examination of the abduction phenomenon' leans on Klass with regard to its earliest recorded instance, that of the

Hills, when he speculates that its more sensational details owe much to subsequent 'research' by the experient: the lady, he thinks, 'was beginning to subconsciously feed into her own recollections some of the data she had picked up from her reading' — though it is not quite clear where and how she got the pertinent material if this is to be regarded as the *first* instance.

Spencer goes on to surmise that the Missing Time Syndrome (so familiar to students of Folklore), in which the percipient is unable to account for 'lost time', was taken aboard the syndrome at this stage. (This may well be so, unless the Wotton case is, as we have suspected, even earlier in its full implications.) Spencer's alternative to a literal acceptance of alien kidnap is plausible as far as it goes. It runs along the lines of the description of the limitations imposed on the inhabitants of the (fictional) *Flatland* of Science Fiction with its two-dimensional inhabitants.

He argues that just as a moth is incapable of comprehending the complexities of the Universe, so Man also is ill-equipped in many respects. On the other hand, his apologies for the inconsistent eccentricities of the aliens who, almost in the same breath, show their complete mastery of modern English (or American), but are not conversant with the names of everyday objects, are less satisfactory. He speculates further that if the phenomenon is basically alien to us and perpetually in a flux, it may be impossible to arrived at a correct model; it might indeed be just 'outside human perspective' or, if you prefer, in an inaccessible part of a carefully concealed strange unknowable dimension (with occasional penetrations of the 'Iron Curtain'.)

In agreement with us, Spencer does not think it impossible that there can be unanswerable questions. We may be loth to admit this humiliating position. We cannot agree too strongly with Vallee when he exhorts us to accept lessons in humility when our knowledge has strict limits and to know all is to know *nothing*. That exceptional authority has concluded that we are face to face with a 'technology' capable of doing serious harm — a sobering thought; leaving us to deplore the passing of the 'days of innocence'.

Much that has been written about military and government cover-ups and involvement is often dismissed as paranoia. We have now reached the stage in our research where we are reluctantly forced to admit that there is a smouldering fire hidden by all that smoke. Ready admittance of ignorance is not on the cards where official institution are concerned. The evidence for alarmingly real physical effects unearthed by Vallee in the course of his investigative journeys goes far beyond an idle rumour and can be ignored at our own peril only. Long before that, it was said that Flying Saucers are 'hostile', but this claim was dismissed as alarmist and cut no ice with serious scholars.

Now in the light of further and deeper research we have to reconsider our stance on this matter, just as we were once forced by the data to abandon the universal entrenched belief in the ET origin of the UFO.

It is said that it is 'unscientific' to discard an hypothesis unless another is at hand to replace it. In the ongoing controversy about the origins of the mysterious crop circles, the meteorological approach seemed promising and more rational than the ufological connection with 'little green men', advocated by the media. But unless it can be shown that there is a water-tight theory to account for the creation of *all* the configurations, that is including the more recent developments with intricate patterns, the case for the natural hypothesis can only be claimed as a possibility, however superior to the more bizarre alternatives some enthusiasts come up with.

Like UFOs and abductions scenarios, the Circles

remain a truly *paranormal* phenomenon in the true sense of the word, which is to say that they are at present inexplicable beyond reasonable doubt. Psychokinetic, and the infinitely more powerful poltergeist, forces come to mind. There is no doubt that these are a fact of nature, less rare than is commonly assumed, whereas the meteorological effects postulated *ad hoc* with much circular reasoning to make them fit a particular theory are unknown and unproved by science.

To sum up. Abductions which contain a strong psychological and sociological element are (rightly or wrongly) attributed to ghost-like semi-physical entities that often cause terror and dismay. They are in the words of Vallee 'Messengers of Deception', whose precise origin and function are obscure and unascertainable. They pretend to arrive in machines of enough variant shapes and sizes to confuse the mind, just as their occupants are inconsistently portrayed with only the slightest concession to taxonomy. Whereas they used to present themselves as would-be Saviours of our planet, they have now abandoned this role in favour of genetic research in medical and biological matters.

They puzzle by their apparent irrationality, but inspire neither confidence nor belief in their much proclaimed superiority at an ethical or technical level. Whether we shall ever be able to unravel these mysteries is an open question, seeing that the phenomenon seems to hail from impenetrable dimensions of enchantment.

BIBLIOGRAPHY

Blackmore S.J., *Beyond the Body*. Heinemann 1982.
Bois, J., *Le Satanisme et la Magie*. Chailly, Paris 1896.
Bowen, C. (ed), *The Humanoids*. N.Spearman, 1969.
Boyd, R.D., *International Who's Who in Ufology Directory*. Southeastern Press, Mobile, Alabama 1988.
Bozzano, E., *Hebersinnliche Erscheinungen*. Francke, Bern 1948
Campbell, S., *Close Encounter at Livingstone*. BUFORA, 1982.
Cassirer, M., *Parapsychology & the UFO*. Cassirer 1988.
Ebon, M., *Exorcism*. Signet Books, New York 1974.
Evans, H., *Visions — Apparitions — Alien Visitors*. Aquarian 1984
Evans, H & Spencer, J., *UFOs 1947 –987*. Fortean Tomes 1987
Ewan, C.L., *Witchcraft & Demonianism*. Cranton 1993.
Falla, G., *Vehicle Interference Project*. BUFORA 1976.
Fodor, N., *An Encyclopedia of Psychic Science*. Citadel 1974.
Fowler, R.E., *The Andreasson Affair*. Bantam Books, New York 1979
Gauld, A. & Cornell, A.D., *Poltergeists*. RPK 1979.
Green, C. & McCreery, C., *Apparitions*. H. Hamilton 1975.
Hendry, A., *The UFO Handbook*. Doubleday, New York 1979.
Hopkins, B., *Intruders*. Sphere Books 1987.

Hufford, D.J., *The Terror That Comes in the Night*. Univ. of Pennsylvania Press 1982
Kalweit, H., *Dreamtime & Inner Space*. Shambhala, Boston 1988.
Keel, J.A., *Strange Creatures from Time & Space*. Fawcett, Brooklyn, N.Y. 1970
Kirk, R., *The Secret Commonwealth*. 1691.
Kittredge, G.L., *Witchcraft in Old & New England*. Harvard Univ. Press 1928.
Klass, P., *UFO-Abductions*. Prometheus, Buffalo, N.Y. 1988
Kramer, H. & Sprenger, J. (ed Summer), *Malleus Maleficarum*. Arrow Books 1971.
Lea, H.C., *History of Witchcraft*. Yoseloff, New York 1957.
Levi, E., *Dogme et Rituel de la haute magi*. Brailliere, Paris, 1861
McCampbell, J.M., *UFOLOGY*. Celestial Arts, Milbrae 1976.
MacKenzie, A., *Hauntings & Apparitions*. Heinemann 1983; *The Seen & Unseen*. Weidenfeld 1987.
Moravec, M., *PSIUFO Phenomena*. Gosford, NSW. 1982
Notestein, W., *A History of Witchcraft in England*. Cromwell, New York 1968
Oesterreich, T.K., *Possession*. K. Paul 1930.
Oasis, K. & Haraldson, E., *At The Hour of Death*. Avon, New York 1972.
Owen, A.R.G., *Can We Explain The Poltergeist?* Garrett Pub. New York 1964
Pocknett, L (ed.), *Encyclopaedia of the Paranormal*. Macmillan 1990
Playfair, G.L., *The Unknown Power*. Panther 1977.
Price, H., *Stella C*. Hurst & Blackett 1925.
Randles, J., *Abductions*. Hale 1988.
Rimmer, J., *Abductions*. Aquarian 1984.
Robbins, R.H., *The Encyclopedia of Withcraft & Demonology*. P. Nevill 1965.
Rochas, A. de, *L'Exteriorisation de la Motricite*. Charconac, Paris 1906
Rodeghier, M., *Vehicle Interference*. CUFOS 1981

Rogo, D.S., *UFO Abductions*. Signet Books, New York 1980.
Rogo, D.S., *Beyond Reality*. Aquarian Press 1990.
Scott, Sir W., *Demonology & Witchcraft*. Routledge 1885.
Stevenson, T., *Twenty Cases Suggestive of Reincarnation*. ASPR., New York 1966
Story, R.D., *The Enclopedia of UFOs*. Doubleday, New York 1980
Spencer, J., *Perspectives*. Macdonald 1989.
Spencer, J. & Evans, H., *Phenomenon*. Futura 1988.
Strieber, W., *Communion*. Arrow Books 1988.
Thurston, H., *The Physical Phenomena of Mysticism*. Burns 1951; *Surprising Mystics*. Burns 1955.
Vallee, J., *Magonia*. Spearman 1970; *UFOs: The Psychic Solution*. Panther, Frogmore 1977; *Dimensions*. Souvenir 1988; *Confrontations*. Souvenir 1988.
Wilson, I., *The Bleeding Mind*. Weidenfeld 1988.
Zucher, E. *Les Apparition d'Humanoids*. Le Feuvre, Nice 1979.